THE
HEALTHY CEO

EMBRACING PHYSICAL, EMOTIONAL, AND MENTAL WELL-BEING

JASON MILLER

CHRIS O'BYRNE,
MARIA MAYES, JON HOERAUF,
ANNA CHOI, DR. DAVID YODER

ISBN: 978-1-957217-39-0 (paperback)
ISBN: 978-1-957217-40-6 (hardback)
ISBN: 978-1-957217-41-3 (ebook)

CONTENTS

The CEO's Guide to Mastering Health and Leadership

Jason Miller

As a CEO and business owner across various industries, I've learned that the cornerstone of effective leadership is not just intellect or business acumen but a robust foundation of physical, emotional, and mental well-being. This realization didn't come to me overnight. Through years of navigating the high-pressure environments of entrepreneurship, I understood the profound impact of health on my ability to lead, innovate, and persevere.

In its comprehensive form, health is the bedrock upon which the pillars of successful leadership rest. It's akin to maintaining a well-oiled machine; every part needs to function optimally for the whole system to work efficiently. For a business leader, physical health is not merely about avoiding sickness. It's about cultivating an energized body ready to tackle the day's challenges. It's about having the stamina to endure long hours when deadlines loom and the resilience to bounce back from setbacks.

1

But physical well-being is just one aspect. Emotional health is equally critical. The entrepreneurial path is one of volatility, with highs that can soar to the sky and lows that can plunge into the abyss. Nurturing emotional well-being allows us to ride these waves gracefully, maintaining our equilibrium in the face of triumphs and trials. It equips us with the empathy to connect with our team members on a human level, fostering a work environment where people feel valued and understood.

Then there's mental health, perhaps the most crucial yet often overlooked component. A clear and focused mind is our greatest asset in the business world. It enables us to think strategically, solve complex problems, and develop innovative solutions. But when mental health is neglected, our cognitive functions suffer, leading to clouded judgment and impaired decision-making. In the fast-paced business world, where every decision can have significant implications, the stakes are too high to ignore this vital aspect of our well-being.

However, recognizing the importance of health is one thing; prioritizing it amid the relentless demands of running a business is another. It's all too easy to fall into the trap of putting health on the back burner, convincing ourselves that we'll focus on it "later" when we have more time. But in the whirlwind of entrepreneurship, "later" often never comes. Before we know it, we're caught in a cycle of stress, fatigue, and diminishing returns, both personally and professionally.

I've been there, caught up in the endless pursuit of success at the expense of my health. But I learned the hard way that neglecting health is a false economy. The time and energy we think we're saving by skipping meals, cutting back on sleep, or ignoring stress are ultimately lost to decreased productivity, creativity, and effectiveness. Worse, it sets a harmful precedent for our teams, implying that sacrificing health is acceptable or even expected in the quest for success.

That's why I've made it my mission to integrate health into the very fabric of my leadership and my companies. I've seen how maintaining a balance of physical, emotional, and mental well-being enhances my performance and positively impacts the entire organization. It leads to a culture of well-being where employees feel supported and encouraged to take care of themselves. This, in turn, boosts morale, reduces turnover, and increases productivity, contributing to the business's overall success.

But how does one maintain this balance? It starts with self-awareness, recognizing the signs of burnout, and taking proactive steps to address them. It requires discipline to make time for exercise, ensure proper nutrition, and get enough sleep. It demands courage to face our emotional vulnerabilities and seek support when needed. And it calls for commitment to practice mindfulness, manage stress, and foster a positive mindset.

As leaders, we are also responsible for modeling this behavior, showing our teams that health is not a luxury but a necessity. By sharing our practices and struggles, we can destigmatize discussions around health, encouraging others to prioritize their well-being. We can implement policies that promote work-life balance, provide resources for mental health support, and create a safe space for employees to express their needs and challenges.

The journey of a CEO or business leader is not just about steering a company to financial success. It's about leading by example, showing that it's possible to achieve professional excellence without compromising on health. By prioritizing our physical, emotional, and mental well-being, we enhance our lives and inspire those around us to do the same. This chapter aims to underscore the paramount importance of health in leadership, offering insights and strategies to maintain this delicate balance. In the end, a healthy leader is the most effective leader, capable of guiding their ship through stormy seas to the shores of success.

In the life of a CEO, every day brings its own set of challenges and decisions. Amidst this whirlwind of responsibilities, maintaining physical health might seem like a daunting task. Yet, it's a crucial element of my daily routine, one that I've come to regard not as a chore but as a vital investment in my personal and professional effectiveness.

My approach to physical well-being is built on the understanding that health is not merely the absence of illness but a state of overall vitality. It's about feeling energized from the moment I wake up until I wind down for the night. To achieve this, I focus on three main pillars: nutrition, exercise, and sleep, each playing a unique role in supporting my physical health.

Nutrition, for me, is about fueling my body with the right kind of energy. I've learned that what I eat directly impacts my performance throughout the day. Hence, I start my day with a balanced breakfast that includes a mix of proteins, fats, and carbohydrates. This meal sets the tone for my energy levels and focus. I also keep hydration in mind, drinking plenty of water to stay alert and avoid the midday slump. Lunch and dinner follow a similar pattern, focusing on whole foods that provide sustained energy rather than quick fixes that lead to crashes. I also make it a point to limit caffeine and sugar intake, as they can disrupt my natural energy balance and sleep patterns.

Exercise is another cornerstone of my routine. Finding time for physical activity amidst a packed schedule was a challenge at first. However, I discovered that integrating exercise into my daily life was less about finding time and more about prioritizing it. I opt for activities that I enjoy, which makes it easier to stay consistent. Whether it's a morning jog, a cycling session, or a workout at the gym, the goal is to get moving and increase my heart rate. This boosts my physical health and clears my mind, making me more productive and creative.

Sleep, often underrated, is perhaps the most critical component of my physical health regimen. The demands of leadership can tempt one to cut back on sleep to get more done. Yet, I've found that sacrificing sleep is counterproductive. It diminishes cognitive function, emotional resilience, and overall health. Therefore, I make it a priority to get seven to eight hours of quality sleep each night. This means creating a conducive sleep environment, free from distractions and blue light from screens, and establishing a regular bedtime routine to signal to my body that it's time to wind down.

Balancing these aspects of physical health hasn't been easy, requiring a shift in perspective. Initially, I saw them as separate from my work, almost like interruptions. Over time, I've come to view them as integral parts of my success as a CEO. Nutrition, exercise, and sleep are not just personal health choices but strategic business decisions. They directly impact my ability to lead, make decisions, and inspire those around me.

Implementing these practices has also taught me the value of self-discipline and routine. By sticking to a schedule for meals, exercise, and sleep, I've developed habits that support my health goals. This discipline translates into my professional life, enhancing my ability to manage time, set priorities, and stay focused on my objectives.

Moreover, maintaining physical health has broader implications for leadership. It sets a positive example for my team, showing that health is a priority at all levels of the organization. It's about leading by example, demonstrating that taking care of one's health is not just important but essential for sustained performance and well-being.

In reflecting on my journey to maintain physical well-being, I recognize that it's an ongoing process. There are days when the balance tips, and I might skip a workout or compromise on sleep due to work demands. However, these are not failures but reminders of the need for flexibility and forgiveness in the pursuit of health. What's important is the commitment to get back on track, learning from each experience and adjusting as needed.

This commitment to physical health is not just about personal benefits. It's a cornerstone of effective leadership, enhancing not just my performance but also contributing to the culture and success of my businesses. It underscores the message that in the fast-paced world of entrepreneurship, taking care of one's health is not a luxury but a necessity.

As I share my routine and insights, I hope to inspire other CEOs and business leaders to prioritize their physical health. It's an invitation to view health not as an obstacle to success but as a fundamental component of it. By investing in our physical well-being, we're not just improving our lives but setting the stage for healthier, more resilient organizations.

Balancing the relentless demands of running a business with the need to stay physically healthy is akin to walking a tightrope. Every day, I'm faced with decisions that test my commitment to my well-being against the backdrop of business goals, meetings, and deadlines. As a CEO and business owner, I've had to navigate this challenging landscape, learning and adapting strategies that allow me to maintain my physical health while steering my companies forward.

When I first embarked on my entrepreneurial journey, I viewed my health and business as competing interests. Time spent exercising or planning healthy meals felt like time stolen from my companies. A flawed perspective led to a cycle of stress, fatigue, and, ultimately, diminished productivity and effectiveness. This experience taught me a valuable lesson: my health is not a separate entity from my business; it is the very foundation upon which my ability to lead and make decisions rests.

The first strategy I adopted was redefining what success meant to me. Success is not just about financial metrics or market share; it's also about leading a balanced life where health is a priority. This shift in mindset was crucial. It allowed me to view time spent on health-related activities not as lost business time but as an investment in my leadership capacity and, by extension, in my company's success.

Integrating physical activity into my daily routine was the next step. I had to be creative and flexible, finding ways to incorporate exercise without it feeling like a burden. I started scheduling walking meetings, which allowed me to stay active and brought a fresh perspective to discussions. I encouraged my team to join me, fostering a culture of health within the company. These walks became a space for open communication, idea sharing, and problem-solving, proving that health and business objectives can indeed complement each other.

Time management played a pivotal role in balancing work and health. I learned to scrutinize my schedule, identifying tasks that could be delegated or meetings that could be shortened or even eliminated. This prioritization process freed up time for health activities without compromising my responsibilities as CEO. It was about making smart choices and recognizing that trying to do everything myself was neither sustainable nor healthy. Delegation benefited my physical health and empowered my team, giving them ownership and responsibility, which in turn drove the company forward.

Setting boundaries was another crucial strategy. In today's connected world, it's easy to fall into the trap of being available 24/7, blurring the lines between work and personal time. I had to establish clear boundaries, dedicating specific times for work and health-related activities. This meant learning to say no, turning off notifications after hours, and communicating these boundaries to my team. It was a challenge at first, but it taught me the importance of rest and recovery, not just for my health but as a tool for enhancing creativity and productivity.

Perhaps the most significant strategy was leading by example. As a CEO, my actions set the tone for the entire organization. By prioritizing my health, I clearly communicated that our company values and respects well-being. This approach led to the implementation of wellness programs, flexible work arrangements, and health-focused team-building activities. It cultivated an environment where employees feel supported in their health goals, which in turn contributes to a more engaged, motivated, and productive workforce.

Reflecting on my journey, I've come to understand that balancing work and health is not a one-time adjustment but an ongoing process of learning and adaptation. There have been times when the balance tipped too far in one direction, requiring me to reassess and recalibrate. These moments, while challenging, were growth opportunities, allowing me to refine my strategies and become a more effective leader.

In sharing my experience, I hope to inspire other CEOs and business leaders to recognize the inseparable link between health and business success. The strategies I've outlined are not prescriptive; they are a starting point and are meant to be adapted to each individual's unique circumstances and goals. The key is to view health as an integral part of leadership and business strategy rather than an optional add-on.

By embracing this holistic approach, we can redefine the meaning of success, leading companies that not only thrive financially but also promote the well-being of those who drive them forward. It's a vision of leadership where balance is not just possible but embraced, creating a legacy of health, happiness, and resilience for ourselves and our organizations.

Navigating the unpredictable waters of entrepreneurship, I've come to understand that emotional well-being is as crucial to a leader as strategy is to a business. The journey is marked by triumphs and setbacks, each carrying the power to uplift or unnerve. Amidst this rollercoaster, cultivating emotional health has been my anchor, allowing me to lead with empathy, resilience, and a clear mind.

In my view, emotional health is the ability to navigate one's feelings, recognizing them as signposts rather than obstacles. It's about maintaining equilibrium in the face of both success and failure, understanding that both are transient. This perspective didn't come easily to me. Like many entrepreneurs, I initially rode the highs and lows with little regard for emotional balance, letting victories inflate my ego and setbacks plunge me into self-doubt. This approach, however, proved unsustainable. It was only through introspection and deliberate practice that I began to cultivate a more balanced emotional landscape.

One of the first steps in this journey was learning to detach my self-worth from my business's performance. The entrepreneurial identity can become so intertwined with the company that any external success or failure feels deeply personal. I had to learn to step back and see myself as separate from my business outcomes. This shift was pivotal. It allowed me to approach challenges with a clearer head and take failures as opportunities for growth rather than personal defeats.

Another key aspect of nurturing my emotional well-being has been embracing vulnerability. The stereotype of the stoic, unflappable leader is a myth. Authentic leadership is about showing up as your full self, with all your strengths and weaknesses. I've learned that it's okay to express doubts and admit when I don't have all the answers. This openness has helped me connect more deeply with my team and created a culture where vulnerability is seen as a strength, not a weakness.

Building a supportive network has been another cornerstone of maintaining my emotional health. Entrepreneurship can be isolating, with the weight of decision-making resting heavily on one's shoulders. I've made it a priority to surround myself with mentors, peers, and friends who understand the entrepreneurial journey. These relationships have provided me with a sounding board, offering perspective and advice when needed. More importantly, they've reminded me that I'm not alone and that the challenges I face are part of a shared experience.

Practicing mindfulness and reflection has also played a critical role in my emotional well-being. Setting aside time each day to be present and to reflect on my feelings and experiences has helped me develop a deeper understanding of myself and my emotional triggers. This practice has enhanced my ability to respond rather than react to situations, giving me the space to choose how I engage with my emotions.

Perhaps the most challenging aspect of nurturing emotional health has been learning to manage stress effectively. The pressure to perform and meet expectations can be overwhelming. I've adopted several strategies to cope with stress, from regular exercise to meditation and setting realistic goals. These practices have improved my emotional resilience, overall health, and productivity.

As I reflect on my journey, I recognize that emotional health is not a destination but a continuous process of growth and adaptation. It requires commitment, awareness, and the willingness to confront uncomfortable truths about oneself. It's a journey that has made me a better leader and a more fulfilled individual.

In sharing my experience, I hope to inspire other CEOs and entrepreneurs to prioritize their emotional well-being. The challenges of leadership are not just strategic or financial; they are deeply human. By cultivating emotional health, we equip ourselves with the resilience, empathy, and clarity needed to navigate the complexities of business and life. It's an investment that pays dividends not just in improved performance and relationships but in a deeper sense of satisfaction and purpose.

As leaders, we can set an example, showing that emotional well-being is integral to success. By taking care of ourselves, we create a ripple effect, fostering a culture where emotional health is valued and supported. This is the legacy I aim to build, one where success is measured not just by what we achieve but by how we navigate the journey.

Throughout my tenure as a CEO and business owner, I have encountered numerous challenges that have tested my emotional resilience. Among these, one particular instance stands out, not just for the stress it inflicted but for the lessons it imparted. This experience revolved around a critical product launch that was met with unexpected technical failures, threatening the company's reputation and shaking our team's confidence.

The product in question was the culmination of years of research and development, a venture that had consumed significant resources and was anticipated to revolutionize our market segment. The excitement within the team and among our stakeholders was palpable as we approached the launch date. However, shortly after release, reports of technical issues began to surface. The problem was more than a minor glitch; it was a fundamental flaw that compromised the product's core functionality.

The immediate aftermath was a whirlwind of emergency meetings, client calls, and media inquiries. The pressure to rectify the situation was immense, matched only by the weight of disappointment I felt. It was a moment that demanded a strategic response and profound emotional resilience.

When faced with this crisis, my first instinct was to retreat into problem-solving mode, to fix the issue at any cost. However, I quickly realized that addressing the technical failure was only part of the solution. The true challenge lay in managing the emotional fallout within the team and among our clients. This realization marked the beginning of a journey that would test and ultimately strengthen my emotional resilience.

The path forward began with acknowledgment. I had to confront the situation head-on, acknowledging the failure not just internally but publicly. This was a humbling process that required me to set aside any defensiveness and open myself up to criticism. By taking responsibility and committing to resolve the issue, we began to rebuild trust with our clients and stakeholders.

Simultaneously, I turned my attention inward to the team that had poured their hearts into this project. The morale was understandably low, with feelings of frustration, disappointment, and doubt pervasive throughout. Recognizing the importance of emotional support, I prioritized engaging with my team openly and empathetically. I shared my disappointment, emphasizing that failure was not a reflection of our worth but an opportunity for growth. Together, we embarked on a collective process of reflection, identifying not just what went wrong but how we could learn from this experience.

This period of introspection and collective resilience-building was transformative. It fostered a sense of unity and purpose within the team, transforming a moment of crisis into a catalyst for growth. We emerged from this experience with a deeper understanding of our strengths and weaknesses, a renewed commitment to our mission, and a more resilient approach to facing challenges.

The technical issue was eventually resolved, and the product was re-launched to critical acclaim. However, the true victory was not in the product's recovery but in our team's resilience. This experience taught us the value of facing adversity with openness, humility, and a willingness to learn. It underscored the importance of emotional resilience in leadership, not just in navigating crises but in fostering a culture of growth, resilience, and adaptability.

Reflecting on this journey, I am reminded of the power of resilience. Emotional resilience is not about avoiding failure or masking vulnerability; it's about embracing these experiences as integral to our growth. It's about leading with empathy, supporting our teams through challenges, and emerging stronger on the other side.

As CEOs and business leaders, we are often celebrated for our successes. However, it is how we navigate setbacks that truly defines our leadership. By cultivating emotional resilience, we enhance our capacity to lead through adversity and inspire those around us to approach challenges with courage, grace, and an unwavering commitment to growth.

This experience, while difficult, was a profound lesson in the importance of emotional resilience in the entrepreneurial journey. It taught me that resilience is not just a personal attribute but a collective strength forged in the fires of adversity and essential for navigating the complexities of business and life.

In the dynamic business world, where each day presents new challenges, maintaining mental health is not just beneficial—it's imperative. My journey as a CEO has taught me that the vigor of one's mental health can significantly influence one's ability to lead, make decisions, and inspire others. The practices I've integrated into my daily life to ensure my mental well-being are not revolutionary, but their consistent application has been transformative.

Mindfulness and meditation have become cornerstones of my mental health routine. Initially, the concept seemed distant from the fast-paced nature of business. However, I discovered that the quiet reflection these practices offer is what I need to counterbalance the chaos. Each morning, before the day's demands encroach upon my peace, I dedicate time to sit in silence, focusing on my breath and allowing my thoughts to pass without judgment. This simple act of presence has significantly improved my concentration, patience, and emotional regulation throughout the day.

Stress management techniques have also been crucial in navigating the pressures of leadership. Recognizing that stress is an inevitable part of entrepreneurship, I've learned to view it not as an enemy but as a signal that demands attention and adjustment. Regular physical activity is a strategy I employ to manage stress; it releases tension and promotes a sense of well-being. Additionally, setting realistic goals and boundaries has helped me manage expectations—both my own and those of the people around me. Learning to say 'no' and understanding the limits of my capacity have been powerful tools in preserving my mental energy.

Another practice that has greatly benefited my mental health is the cultivation of hobbies outside of work. Unrelated to my business endeavors, these activities serve as an outlet for creative expression and personal fulfillment. Whether painting, hiking, or playing a musical instrument, engaging in hobbies helps me disconnect from work-related thoughts and immerse myself in the joy of the moment. This balance between professional obligations and personal interests has been key to maintaining a healthy mental state.

One of the most significant steps I've taken to promote mental health is fostering open conversations about it within my organizations. By sharing my own experiences and strategies for managing mental well-being, I've aimed to destigmatize mental health issues and encourage others to prioritize their psychological well-being. Creating an environment where employees feel supported in discussing and addressing their mental health challenges is vital. It not only enhances individual well-being but also contributes to a healthier, more productive workplace.

In addition to these personal practices, seeking professional support when needed has been instrumental. Sometimes, the weight of decision-making, leadership responsibilities, and the constant drive for success can become overwhelming. In such moments, consulting with a therapist or counselor has provided me with objective insights, coping strategies, and a deeper understanding of my mental processes. This external perspective is invaluable, offering clarity and guidance that supports my mental health and leadership effectiveness.

Reflecting on my journey, I realize that maintaining mental health is an ongoing process of awareness, action, and adaptation. It requires a commitment to oneself, a willingness to confront challenges, and the humility to seek help when necessary. As a CEO, I've learned that my mental well-being is not just a personal matter; it directly impacts my ability to lead, inspire, and drive my companies forward.

The integration of mindfulness, stress management, hobbies, open conversations about mental health, and professional support into my life has not been without its challenges. However, the benefits—increased clarity, resilience, and a deeper connection with myself and others—far outweigh the difficulties. These practices have not only enhanced my mental health but have also enriched my life in profound ways.

My message to fellow CEOs and business leaders is clear: prioritize your mental health as diligently as you do your business. The strength of your mental well-being is a critical asset in your leadership toolkit, enabling you to navigate business complexities with insight, empathy, and resilience. By adopting practices that support mental health, you invest in your well-being, set a powerful example for your team, and contribute to a culture that values and nurtures mental health at all levels of the organization.

In my journey as a CEO and leader of several companies, I've come to understand that the road to success is rarely traveled alone. The support systems—both personal and professional—that surround me have been instrumental in navigating the complexities of business and leadership. These support networks have provided guidance and encouragement and have also been a source of strength during challenging times.

My support system, comprising family and close friends, has been my bedrock. These are the people who know me beyond the titles and the boardrooms, seeing me for who I am, not just what I do. Their unwavering belief in me, especially during moments of doubt, has been a constant reminder of my worth and potential, separate from my professional achievements. Family dinners, weekend outings, and candid conversations about life's ups and downs have kept me grounded, reminding me that there is a world outside the office that is equally deserving of my time and energy.

Equally important has been my professional support network, consisting of mentors, peers, and trusted colleagues. These relationships have been built over years of shared experiences, successes, and setbacks. With their wealth of experience, my mentors have offered invaluable advice, helping me navigate uncharted territories with their insights and wisdom. Conversations with peers facing similar challenges and aspirations have provided a sense of camaraderie and mutual understanding that is hard to find elsewhere. Meanwhile, my colleagues, with whom I work closely daily, have inspired and motivated me. Their dedication, creativity, and commitment to our shared vision have propelled our companies forward, making each success a collective achievement.

These support systems have played a crucial role during particularly challenging times. I recall a period when one of my companies faced a critical financial crisis that threatened its very existence. The stress and pressure of steering the company through this storm were immense. During this time, the value of my support networks became unequivocally clear. My family provided the emotional support I needed to maintain my resilience, reminding me of the importance of maintaining balance and perspective. My mentors and peers offered strategic advice and shared their experiences of overcoming similar hurdles, giving me the confidence to make tough decisions. My colleagues' commitment to overcoming the crisis reinforced my belief in our collective ability to navigate through adversity.

This experience taught me the importance of leaning on others, being open to receiving support, and the strength that comes from vulnerability. It underscored the fact that leadership is not about going it alone or bearing the weight of challenges in isolation. Rather, it's about recognizing the power of collaboration, mutual support, and shared purpose. It also highlighted the importance of nurturing these support systems, investing time and energy into these relationships, and giving back as much as I have received.

Building and maintaining these support networks requires effort and intentionality. It involves showing appreciation, actively listening, and being there for others, just as they are there for me. It means being honest about my struggles and successes and sharing my journey in a way that invites connection and mutual support. It also requires a willingness to seek help when needed, to admit that I don't have all the answers, and to embrace the collective wisdom and strength of those around me.

As I reflect on the role of support systems in maintaining overall well-being, I am reminded of the African proverb,

"If you want to go fast, go alone. If you want to go far, go together." This adage resonates deeply with my own experience as a CEO. The journey of leadership and entrepreneurship is a marathon, not a sprint. It is fraught with challenges that test our resilience, determination, and integrity. However, with a strong personal and professional support network, these challenges become opportunities for growth, learning, and deeper connection.

In sharing my experience, I hope to inspire other leaders to recognize and value the support systems in their lives. Whether it's family, friends, mentors, or colleagues, these relationships are vital to our well-being and success. They provide a foundation of strength, encouragement, and perspective that enriches our lives and empowers us to achieve our goals. As leaders, we have the privilege and responsibility to foster a culture of support and collaboration within our organizations and broader communities. By doing so, we enhance our well-being and contribute to a more connected, resilient, and supportive society.

As a CEO who has navigated the ebbs and flows of the business world, I've come to recognize the profound impact a company's culture can have on its success. Promoting a culture of health within an organization is not merely a nice-to-have; it's a strategic imperative that benefits everyone involved—employees, leaders, and stakeholders alike. My commitment to fostering a healthy workplace has led to the implementation of several initiatives and policies that encourage well-being among our team members.

The journey to instilling a culture of health began with a simple yet powerful realization: the well-being of our employees directly influences their productivity, creativity, and satisfaction at work. This understanding prompted a shift in how we approached health and wellness within the company. We moved beyond viewing it as solely the responsibility of the individual and started to see it as a collective goal, integral to our organizational identity and values.

One of the first steps we took was to introduce comprehensive wellness programs catering to our employees' physical, mental, and emotional health. These programs include access to fitness facilities, mental health days, and workshops on topics such as stress management, nutrition, and mindfulness. By providing these resources, we aim to empower our team members to take charge of their health and well-being, recognizing that a healthy employee is a happy and productive one.

We also reevaluated our work environment, making changes to promote a healthier, more vibrant workspace. This involved introducing ergonomic furniture, ensuring ample natural light, and creating dedicated relaxation spaces where employees can unwind and recharge. Additionally, we encouraged active breaks and walking meetings to integrate movement into the workday, combating the sedentary lifestyle that often accompanies office jobs.

Flexibility in work arrangements has been another key aspect of our culture shift. Recognizing our employees' diverse needs and life circumstances, we've implemented policies that allow for flexible hours and remote work. This approach acknowledges that work-life balance is critical to health and well-being, and it gives our team members the autonomy to manage their professional and personal responsibilities in a way that suits them best.

Perhaps the most significant change has been in our approach to leadership and communication. We've worked to create an open, inclusive environment where employees feel comfortable discussing their health and well-being. Regular check-ins, anonymous feedback channels, and wellness surveys have been instrumental in this process, allowing us to understand the needs and concerns of our team and adjust our strategies accordingly.

Moreover, we've made a concerted effort to lead by example. As a CEO, I openly share my practices and challenges related to health and well-being, demonstrating that taking care of oneself is not only acceptable but encouraged. This transparency has helped normalize conversations around health in the workplace and has shown our team that their well-being is a priority at the highest levels of the organization.

These initiatives have not been without their challenges. Implementing a culture change requires time, resources, and a willingness to adapt based on feedback. However, the benefits have far outweighed the difficulties. We've observed a marked improvement in employee morale, a decrease in absenteeism, and an increase in overall productivity. Perhaps most importantly, we've seen a stronger sense of community and support among our team members, reinforcing the idea that we are all in this together.

In reflecting on our journey to promote a culture of health within our organizations, I am reminded of the broader impact such efforts can have. By prioritizing the well-being of our employees, we not only enhance their lives but also set a positive example for other companies to follow. We contribute to a shift in societal norms around work and health, advocating for a world where the two are not in conflict but in harmony.

The advice I would offer to other CEOs and business leaders looking to instill a culture of health within their organizations is simple: start with empathy. Understand the needs and challenges of your team and approach health as a shared responsibility. Be willing to invest in the resources and changes needed to support well-being, and remember that the benefits will extend far beyond the immediate impact on health. A culture of health fosters engagement, loyalty, and a sense of purpose, driving the success of not only individuals but of the organization as a whole.

My commitment to promoting a healthy workplace remains unwavering as we move forward. I believe that by prioritizing our employees' well-being, we can build resilient, innovative, and compassionate organizations that thrive economically and as communities of individuals who support and care for one another. This is the legacy I aim to leave as a leader: a testament to the power of prioritizing health in the pursuit of business excellence.

As I reflect on my journey as a CEO and entrepreneur, navigating through the complexities of leadership and the relentless pursuit of success, I've come to understand the indispensable value of health—physical, emotional, and mental. This understanding was not innate; it was forged through experiences, challenges, and the realization that health is not just a personal asset but a cornerstone of effective leadership.

To my fellow CEOs and entrepreneurs, I offer this advice, borne of lessons learned and battles fought in the realm of business and health. Prioritizing your well-being is not a luxury or an afterthought; it is essential to your success and longevity in the demanding world of leadership.

First and foremost, recognize that health and success are not mutually exclusive; they are deeply interconnected. The vitality of your body, the resilience of your emotions, and the clarity of your mind each play a critical role in your ability to lead, make decisions, and inspire those around you. Neglecting any aspect of your health compromises your well-being and the health of your organization.

Embrace a holistic approach to health. Physical fitness, nutritious eating, and sufficient rest are foundational, as are the practices that nurture your emotional and mental well-being. Cultivate habits such as mindfulness, meditation, or journaling to maintain mental clarity. Foster relationships and hobbies outside of work to enrich your emotional life. These practices are not signs of weakness but indicators of a balanced and thoughtful leader.

Learn to set boundaries. The demands of leadership can be all-consuming, but setting limits on your work and allowing time for rest and recuperation are critical for maintaining health. Be deliberate in disconnecting from work, both physically and digitally, to recharge fully. This discipline will not only enhance your health but also improve your productivity and creativity when you are working.

Seek and offer support. Leadership can be a lonely journey, but it doesn't have to be. Build a network of peers, mentors, and professionals who understand the unique pressures of entrepreneurship. Be open about your challenges and seek advice when needed. Similarly, create an environment within your organization where health is openly discussed and support readily available. This culture of mutual care and understanding will strengthen your team and enhance your company's resilience.

Lead by example. Your actions and attitudes toward health set the tone for your organization. Prioritize your well-being openly, and integrate health-positive policies and practices into your company's culture. Whether implementing flexible working arrangements, offering wellness programs, or simply encouraging breaks and physical activity, your commitment to health will inspire those around you to prioritize their well-being.

Finally, embrace the journey. Your path to integrating health into your life and leadership will be unique and filled with successes and setbacks. Each challenge is an opportunity to learn, grow, and refine your approach. Celebrate your successes, however small, and learn from the setbacks. Remember, the goal is not perfection but progress toward a healthier, more balanced life.

In closing, I urge you to consider health not just as one aspect of your life but as a foundational element of your success as a CEO and entrepreneur. The strength of your leadership is built upon the well-being of your body, mind, and spirit. By prioritizing your health, you enhance your life and set a powerful example for your team, your organization, and the broader business community.

The journey of leadership is demanding, but it is also immensely rewarding. Integrating health into your leadership's fabric opens the door to a more fulfilling, impactful, and sustainable career. This is the legacy I strive to build and the message I hope to share: that health and success in business and life are not just compatible—they are inseparable.

About the Author

Jason Miller is an accomplished business leader with over thirty years of experience, renowned for his expertise in hyper company growth, scaling, and strategic and operational implementation. He founded the Strategic Advisor Board (SAB) in 2017 and served as its Senior Global Council Member, overseeing its global operations and team capabilities. In addition to his primary role at SAB, Jason holds multiple chair positions across various companies and nonprofits. He has built more than twenty-four companies from scratch since 2001 and is dedicated to crafting sustainable business models emphasizing leadership responsibility, strategy, and accountability.

Known for his no-excuses approach and nicknamed "The Bull," Jason has advised thousands of global leaders. He has been recognized as a foremost expert in consulting for creating scalable business models, particularly for small and mid-market companies. His focus extends to fostering a positive company culture, enhancing staff retention, and deepening customer loyalty, believing that a clear vision and purpose are essential for impactful business. As a veteran, Jason is committed to serving veteran-owned companies and provides pro bono services to veteran organizations as part of a five-year plan.

Jason holds an MBA from Trident University and credits the "school of hard knocks" for his doctorate in practical experience. He is affiliated with numerous prestigious organizations that impact business globally, such as the American Club Association, Leigh Steinberg Academy, Forbes Council, and Entrepreneur Magazine Leadership Council. A lifetime member of the American Legion, Disabled American Veterans, and Veterans of Foreign Wars, Jason lives in Boulder, Colorado, with his family. He focuses on professional development and business strategy to serve his clients better.

Running Your Business without Running Out of Steam

Chris O'Byrne

Let's face it, being at the helm of a business isn't just about making tough decisions, crunching numbers, or sealing deals. It's also about running a marathon at sprint speed, juggling chainsaws while balancing on a tightrope. And guess what? You can't do any of that if you're not in top-notch shape—physically, emotionally, and mentally. So, why is prioritizing our health as crucial as making our next business move? Well, let me tell you.

First off, our bodies are like our businesses' most valuable assets. Imagine trying to run your company with a fleet of rundown, sputtering vehicles. Not very efficient, right? That's what neglecting our physical health does to us. It's like expecting peak performance from a clunker that hasn't seen a service station in years. We need to be in good shape to keep up with the demands of leadership, from enduring back-to-back meetings to surviving those red-eye flights.

But it's not just about the physical. Oh no, the plot thickens. Our emotional and mental well-being are the silent partners in this venture, often overlooked but crucial to our success. Ever tried to make a critical decision while feeling like an emotional pinball machine? Or brainstorm the next big idea when your mind is as foggy as a winter morning in San Francisco? Spoiler alert: It doesn't end well.

Prioritizing our health isn't a luxury; it's a necessity. It keeps us sharp, resilient, and ready to face whatever plot twist our business throws at us. And let's be honest, in the world of entrepreneurship, plot twists are as common as coffee meetings. By taking care of ourselves, we're not just investing in our well-being; we're investing in our company's future. Because, at the end of the day, a healthy CEO is at the heart of a thriving business.

So, as we embark on this journey together, let's remember that embracing our health is not just about avoiding sickness. It's about enhancing our capacity to lead, innovate, and inspire. It's about showing up as the best version of ourselves for our teams, our customers, and, most importantly, for us. After all, you wouldn't expect to win a race with a flat tire, would you? Let's pump up those tires, fuel up, and get ready to lead the pack.

* * *

When it comes to keeping this machine—also known as my body—in tip-top shape, I've got a routine that might make less sense than a hedge fund manager's investment strategy, but trust me, it works. It's not about being a marathon runner or a vegan guru; it's about finding a balance that keeps you feeling like a well-oiled machine, even if sometimes that machine feels more like an old pickup truck than a sports car.

My day starts with what I call a "sunrise surprise." This isn't a fancy drink or a secret yoga pose; it's simply getting out of bed when the sun does, which, depending on the time of year, can be a surprise in itself. The early morning is when I do my best thinking, planning, and sweating. Exercise for me isn't about lifting weights that weigh more than a small car or running until I'm a human puddle. It's about moving, stretching, and telling my body, *Hey, we've got a big day ahead, so let's get the engines running.*

Then there's the fuel I put into this high-performance machine. I'm not talking about downing kale smoothies like they're going out of style or munching on quinoa as if it's popcorn. No, my diet is all about moderation. It's about enjoying that steak but also making sure I'm not treating vegetables like they're poisonous. And hydration—let's not forget about that. I drink water like it's my job, which, considering how much better I think, plan, and act when I'm well-hydrated, it kind of is.

Sleep, oh glorious sleep. It's the unsung hero of my physical health routine. In a world where burning the midnight oil is often worn as a badge of honor, I treat sleep like the golden ticket to productivity. Seven to eight hours is the magic number. Any less, and I'm as useful as a screen door on a submarine. Any more, and I might as well start the day in my pajamas because that's where my energy levels will be.

So, there you have it. My strategy for maintaining physical health might not make headlines or become the next fitness craze, but it's about consistency, balance, and listening to what my body needs. It's about remembering that, as a CEO, I'm in it for the long haul, and keeping this body running smoothly is key to making sure I cross that finish line with my arms raised high, even if I'm secretly dreaming of a nap and a pizza.

* * *

Balancing the demands of running a business while staying physically healthy is like juggling flaming torches while riding a unicycle. It sounds impossible, and you're pretty sure you'll get burned, but you find your rhythm with practice.

The secret sauce (and no, I'm not talking about the kind you find on a Big Mac) to maintaining this balance is setting non-negotiables. These are the things in my life I don't compromise on, come hell or high water. For instance, no matter how chaotic my schedule looks, I carve out time for exercise. It might mean waking up when the only people awake are bakers and insomniacs, but that's a sacrifice I'm willing to make. This time isn't just about keeping fit; it's my sanctuary, a time when I can clear my head and prepare for the day's battles.

Then there's the art of saying no. In the early days, I treated "yes" like it was going out of style. Yes to every meeting, yes to every project, yes to every late-night email. But I quickly learned that saying yes to everything meant saying no to my health and well-being. So, I became more selective, treating my time like the precious commodity it is. It's not about being selfish; it's about being strategic. You can't pour from an empty cup, and you certainly can't run a business if you're running on empty.

Delegation is another key player in my balancing act. Initially, I clung to tasks like a toddler with a favorite toy, convinced no one could do them as well as I could. But that's the fastest route to Burnout City, population: me. Learning to trust my team and pass the baton was a game-changer. It freed up my time to focus on my health and empowered my team, boosting their skills and confidence.

Lastly, I integrate health into my workday. Who says meetings can only happen in stuffy conference rooms? Walking meetings are a revelation—fresh air, a change of scenery, and the chance to stretch my legs. And lunch breaks? They're not just for scarfing down food at my desk. I use them to recharge, whether it's a quick workout or simply stepping outside to soak up some vitamin D.

Finding the balance between work and health is an ongoing journey filled with trial and error. Some days, I feel like a circus performer who's nailed the routine. On other days, it's a miracle if I don't drop all the torches. But the key is persistence, learning from each stumble, and remembering that my health is the foundation upon which my business is built. Without it, everything else crumbles.

* * *

Navigating the emotional roller coaster of entrepreneurship is like being strapped into the world's most unpredictable ride, blindfolded. One minute, you're on top of the world; the next, you're convinced your business is a house of cards on the verge of collapse. It's thrilling, terrifying, and a bit mad. So, how do I keep my emotional health from resembling a ship in a storm? It's all about anchoring myself to practices that keep me steady, even when the waves hit.

First up, perspective. It's my secret weapon. When things go sideways, as they inevitably do, I take a step back and ask myself, "Will this matter in five years?" More often than not, the answer is no. This simple question helps me shrink mountains back into molehills and keeps my emotional energy focused on what truly matters. It's like having a mental dimmer switch, turning down the moment's intensity so I can see the bigger picture.

Then there's the power of laughter. Yes, you heard that right. In the face of stress, my go-to strategy is finding humor in the chaos. It might sound counterintuitive, but laughing in the eye of the storm is incredibly grounding. It's a reminder not to take myself too seriously. After all, if I can find something to chuckle about when the chips are down, it's a small victory against the day's dramas. Plus, it's hard to be stressed when you're busy laughing at the absurdity of a situation or, more often, at yourself.

Emotional health for me also means leaning into vulnerability. There's a strength in admitting you don't have all the answers, that sometimes, you're just winging it. Early on, I thought I had to be this unflappable leader, a stoic figurehead immune to doubt. Spoiler alert: That's a one-way ticket to Burnoutville. Opening up, whether to a trusted friend, a mentor, or my team, has not only lightened my emotional load but also fostered deeper connections. It turns out that vulnerability is less about exposing weaknesses and more about building bridges.

Lastly, I make time for what lights me up outside of work. Whether strumming my guitar, losing myself in a good book, or just pottering around in the garden, these moments of joy are my emotional lifelines. They're reminders that my identity isn't tied solely to my business. I'm a multifaceted human being with interests, passions, and quirks that exist outside the boardroom.

Cultivating emotional health is an ongoing process, a daily commitment to myself. It's about recognizing that the ups and downs are part of the journey, learning to ride the waves with grace, and maybe, just maybe, enjoying the ride.

* * *

There was this one time, in the thick of my entrepreneurial journey, when my emotional resilience was tested more than a high school senior during finals week. Picture this: A major deal, one that had been in the works for months, the kind that could catapult my business from the minor leagues to the majors, suddenly fell through. And not in a quiet, "let's just move on" kind of way. No, it crashed and burned spectacularly, taking a chunk of my confidence with it.

In the immediate aftermath, I felt like I was the captain of a sinking ship, watching as water gushed in, with no idea how to plug the leaks. Doubt, fear, and a sense of failure swirled around me like a personal storm cloud. It was my make-or-break moment, a test of emotional resilience I wasn't sure I was prepared for.

So, what did I do? I did what any self-respecting entrepreneur would do: I allowed myself a pity party. Yes, for a brief moment, I wallowed. I'm talking about a full-on "woe is me" extravaganza. But here's the thing about pity parties: They're like soda. A few sips might taste sweet, but if you drink too much, you'll feel sick.

Once the party was over, I dusted myself off and took a hard look in the mirror. I realized that if I was going to get through this, I needed to harness every ounce of resilience I had. So, I started with acceptance. I acknowledged the failure, not as a reflection of my worth but as a single event. A plot twist in my entrepreneurial saga, if you will.

Next, I reached out to my support network. I'm talking about the kind of friends who don't just offer a shoulder to cry on but also give you the metaphorical slap you need to snap out of it. They reminded me of my past successes, my strengths, and, most importantly, that failure wasn't the end of the story. It was just a chapter.

Armed with renewed determination, I began to strategize. I dissected the failed deal, learning from the missteps and identifying growth opportunities. This wasn't about assigning blame but about understanding and evolving. I realized that resilience isn't just about bouncing back; it's about bouncing forward, using the experience as a springboard for future success.

Looking back, that period of emotional turmoil was a turning point. It taught me that resilience is not inherent; it's built through trials and tribulations. It's about facing setbacks head-on, allowing yourself to feel the disappointment, but then, crucially, finding a way to rise above it.

So, to any entrepreneur facing a moment of doubt, remember this: Emotional resilience is your secret weapon. It's what transforms a setback into a setup for a comeback. And trust me, when you make that comeback, it'll feel like winning the World Series, even if you're the only one in the stands cheering.

* * *

Maintaining mental health is my secret script in the grand theater of entrepreneurship, where every day feels like an opening night with no rehearsals. It's the difference between delivering a standing ovation performance and getting booed off the stage by my brain. So, how do I keep my mental game Oscar-worthy? Let me pull back the curtain.

First, mindfulness is my leading actor. Before you imagine me sitting cross-legged atop a mountain, let me clarify. My mindfulness practice is as down-to-earth as it gets. It's about being present in the moment, whether savoring that first sip of coffee in the morning or truly listening to a team member without mentally rehearsing my to-do list. This simple act of being present cuts through the noise, reduces stress, and keeps my mental chatter from turning into a full-blown monologue.

Then there's meditation, my supporting actor. Ten minutes a day is all it takes. Just me, a quiet space and an attempt to clear my mind, which often feels like trying to herd cats. But here's the kicker: It works. It's like hitting the reset button on my brain, giving me clarity and calmness amid chaos. And on days when my thoughts do resemble unruly felines, I remind myself that the effort itself is a victory.

Stress management techniques are my special effects crew. They add the dazzle and keep the drama on screen, not in my head. Exercise is a big one. It's not just about physical health; it's my mental escape hatch. Whether it's a brisk walk, a sweaty run, or a bout with the punching bag, moving my body is like shaking off the mental cobwebs, making room for creativity and problem-solving.

But here's the plot twist: I also embrace boredom. Yes, you heard that right. In a world that glorifies busyness, I've found magic in stillness. Those moments of nothingness, like staring out the window or watching the clouds, are when my brain gets to breathe. It's when my best ideas waltz in, unannounced but always welcome.

Lastly, I've learned the art of saying "goodnight" to my gadgets. An hour before bed, I turn off my screens, silencing the constant ping of notifications. This digital detox is my mental health nightcap, helping me wind down and ensuring my sleep is as restorative as possible.

So, there you have it. My mental health toolkit might not be revolutionary, but it's tailored to fit the ups and downs of my entrepreneurial journey. It's about finding balance, embracing simplicity, and remembering that, in the end, my mental health is the real MVP of my success story.

* * *

In the epic saga of entrepreneurship, where every day feels like navigating through a jungle with a blindfold, my support systems are my compass and machete. They're the unsung heroes, the backstage crew that keeps the show running smoothly. Let me introduce you to the cast.

First, there's the family ensemble. Picture a group of individuals who've seen me at my best and worst yet inexplicably choose to stick around. They're the ones who remind me that there's life beyond spreadsheets and pitch decks. Whether it's a well-timed joke to lighten the mood or a shared meal where business talk is banned, they ground me. They're a living, breathing reminder that success isn't just measured in profit margins but in moments of genuine connection.

Then there's the band of mentors. These are the seasoned veterans, the wise sages who've been through the wars and have the scars to prove it. They offer guidance, a listening ear, and, sometimes, a much-needed reality check. It's like having a personal board of advisors, except they're less interested in dividends and more in my development. Their wisdom is a lighthouse, guiding me through stormy seas and preventing me from crashing into the rocks of bad decisions.

Let's not forget the fellowship of peers—other entrepreneurs who are in the trenches, fighting their own battles. There's a camaraderie in shared struggle, a sense of solidarity that's hard to find elsewhere. We swap war stories, share resources, and sometimes, just vent. It's a reminder that I'm not alone on this journey and that others understand the unique blend of exhilaration and exhaustion that comes with building something from the ground up.

And, of course, there's the squad of professionals. Think therapists, coaches, and wellness experts. They're the pit crew in my race, ensuring I'm mentally and emotionally tuned for performance. They offer strategies, tools, and, most importantly, a space to unpack the mental luggage that inevitably accumulates. With their help, I've learned to navigate my inner landscape, recognizing that self-awareness is a superpower in the world of business.

Each member of this support system plays a crucial role, offering different guidance, relief, or encouragement. They remind me that while entrepreneurship is often glorified as a solo journey, the truth is far from it. It's a team sport, and my team is eclectic, diverse, and utterly indispensable.

So, to any entrepreneur feeling like they're navigating this jungle alone, remember that building a support system is not a sign of weakness but a strategy for resilience. It's about surrounding yourself with people who can see the forest for the trees, even when you're lost among the branches. With them by your side, the path forward is a little less daunting and a lot more doable.

* * *

As the captain of this somewhat erratic ship called my business, I've learned that the health of my crew is just as crucial as my own. After all, a ship is only as strong as its crew, and a business is only as vibrant as its team. So, how do I promote a culture of health within my organization? It's not by turning the office into a gym or replacing all meals with kale smoothies; I'll tell you that much.

First, I lead by example. You won't catch me bragging about pulling all-nighters or skipping meals to meet deadlines. Instead, I'm the guy championing reasonable work hours, taking lunch breaks, and, yes, even using my vacation days. It's about showing my team that health isn't a luxury; it's a necessity. If I'm preaching wellness but living like a hermit with a caffeine IV, what message does that send?

Next, I've made wellness a part of our conversation, not just a footnote in our employee handbook. We talk about mental health with the same openness as project deadlines. It's about creating an environment where taking a mental health day is as normal as taking a day off for a cold. This openness doesn't just happen overnight. It's like trying to start a lawnmower that's been sitting in the shed all winter. It takes a few pulls, some patience, and maybe a little cursing, but eventually, it gets going.

Then there's the part where I put my money where my mouth is. We've introduced wellness initiatives that don't just look good on paper but make a difference. Think flexible working arrangements, meditation sessions, and yes, even nutrition workshops that don't end with a sales pitch for a diet plan. It's about providing resources and opportunities for my team to take charge of their health in a way that fits their needs and lifestyles.

But here's the kicker: I also encourage fun. Yes, fun—the thing that often gets lost in the sea of deadlines and meetings. We've got a company sports team (and by sports, I mean anything that doesn't require us to be the next Olympic squad), group outings, and even a gaming night. It's about reminding my team that health isn't just about avoiding illness; it's about enjoying life, building connections, and, dare I say, having a good laugh.

Creating a culture of health within an organization is like planting a garden. It requires care, patience, and a bit of trial and error. But the sense of achievement is unparalleled when you see the first sprouts of change. It's about cultivating an environment where everyone can thrive, not just survive. And if that means I have to lead the charge by swapping my coffee for water or taking a walk during a meeting, then so be it. After all, a healthy crew makes for a smooth sailing ship, and I'm all about navigating these waters with as little drama as possible.

* * *

If you think running a business is a smooth ride, let me introduce you to my friend Reality. He's a bit of a party crasher. There was this one time, not too long ago, when Reality threw a wrench in my well-oiled machine, testing my patience and my health. Picture this: A product launch that I had poured my heart, soul, and countless hours into flopped—not just a small stumble but a face-first dive into the mud.

In the aftermath, I felt like a deflated balloon after a party. The energy and enthusiasm I had for my work were sapped. My physical health took a nosedive, too. Stress eating became my new hobby, and the gym felt like a distant memory. Sleep? Let's just say I was more familiar with the late-night TV schedule than I'd like to admit.

But here's the thing about setbacks—they're not just obstacles; they're opportunities. Opportunities to learn, grow, and even laugh a little at the absurdity of it all. So, after my brief stint as a nocturnal creature, I decided it was time to bounce back. But how?

First, I took a step back to breathe and assess. I looked at the situation not as a failure but as a learning experience. What went wrong? What could I have done differently? This wasn't about wallowing in self-pity but about conducting a post-mortem with a clear head. It was like detective work without the cool hat and magnifying glass.

Next, I focused on rebuilding my routine. Slowly but surely, I reintroduced exercise, not as a punishment but as a way to clear my mind and boost my mood. I swapped the late-night snacks for meals that didn't come out of a vending machine. And sleep? I made it my new best friend, setting a strict bedtime routine that even a toddler would envy.

But the real game-changer was reconnecting with my why. Why did I start this business? What was my mission? As painful as it was, this setback reminded me of my passion and drive. It was like finding my north star amid a storm.

And let's not forget the power of support. Leaning on friends, family, and mentors helped me see that this setback wasn't the end of the world. They offered perspective, advice, and the occasional kick in the pants to get me moving forward.

Looking back, I realize that setback was a turning point. It taught me resilience, humility, and the importance of health—not just as a CEO but as a human being. It showed me that setbacks aren't just hurdles but steps to something greater.

So, to any entrepreneur staring down the barrel of a setback, remember this: It's not the fall that defines you, but how you choose to get back up. And sometimes, the best way to get back up is with a good night's sleep, a healthy meal, and a reminder of why you started this journey in the first place.

* * *

As I sit here, reflecting on the rollercoaster ride that is entrepreneurship, I can't help but think about what advice I'd give to fellow CEOs and business leaders. It's not about revealing some secret formula hidden in the vaults of successful CEOs. Nope, it's about sharing the nitty-gritty, the lessons learned from the trenches of business warfare. So, grab a seat, maybe a snack, and let's dive into the wisdom I've gathered, minus the corporate jargon.

First, embrace the trifecta of physical, emotional, and mental health. Think of them as the three musketeers of your well-being. Neglect one, and you're essentially fighting with one hand tied behind your back. Keep moving, find joy in the little things, and don't let your brain bully you into thinking you're invincible. Spoiler alert: You're human, and that's perfectly okay.

Next, remember that balance isn't a myth, and it's also not a one-size-fits-all. Your version of balance might look like a well-orchestrated symphony, while someone else's resembles a jazz improvisation. Find what works for you and run with it. And by run, I mean walk, because remember, we're all about that balance.

Now, let's talk about the power of saying no. It's a tiny word, but boy, does it pack a punch. Saying no to one thing means you're saying yes to something else—like your health, family, or that hobby you've been neglecting. Think of no as your personal bouncer, keeping out the things that don't serve your well-being or your business.

Don't forget to build your support squad. This isn't just about networking; it's about creating a community of people who get it. The ones you can call at 2:00 a.m. when you're on the verge of a breakthrough or a breakdown. These are your people, your tribe. Cherish them, lean on them, and be there for them too.

Lastly, make time for reflection and laughter. Yes, laughter. If you can't laugh at the absurdity of some situations, you're missing out on a crucial stress-relief tool. Reflect on your journey, the highs, the lows, and everything in between. In these moments of reflection, you'll find clarity, gratitude, and maybe even inspiration for your next big move.

So, there you have it, my pearls of wisdom. Take them with a grain of salt or a shot of tequila, whichever you prefer. The journey of a CEO is as much about leading a business as it is about leading a life worth living. And at the end of the day, it's not just about the empire you build but the person you become in the process. Cheers to that.

ABOUT THE AUTHOR

Chris O'Byrne is the CEO of Jetlaunch Publishing and has published over 15,000 books in seventeen years. He has published books for people such as John Lee Dumas, Ed Mylett, Rachel Pedersen, Joe Vitale, and Kary Oberbrunner.

Chris has created over one hundred partnerships and has 16 international bestsellers to his name. He is the editor-in-chief of the influential business magazine, *Pivot Magazine*, which reaches millions in distribution and has featured business and leadership influencers such as Robert Kiyosaki of Rich Dad, General Petreaus (former director of the CIA), and Joe Foster, founder of Reebok.

Explode your business growth with:

Your Million-Dollar Book
yourmilliondollarbook.pro

(Sign up to receive a free book audit.)

THE FULLY ALIVE CEO

MARIA MAYES

Each of us possesses a unique perspective about what it means to be healthy. In the West, health is often oversimplified to mean not having any injuries or diseases, but I believe it's much more comprehensive. True health is a state of complete integration where our bodies, minds, and spirits are in sync. This alignment brings about a dynamic state of health characterized by an energetic body capable of moving freely and with ease.

Achieving health means acknowledging that we transcend mere physical existence. It entails cultivating self-awareness and embracing profound self-compassion, enabling us to extend empathy more wholly to others. A state of health also entails maintaining an alert and reflective mind, understanding that we are distinct from our thoughts—we are the observers of our thoughts, not defined by them.

In essence, health is the experience of being fully alive to every potential and opportunity. It is a state of joy, a resonance that life is not just about the absence of illness but about the presence of well-being and embracing each vibrant moment.

* * *

A healthy CEO embodies a model of wholeness, combining self-awareness with self-compassion. This leader understands that nurturing the body, mind, and spirit is essential and that balance among them is fundamental. Recognizing the presence of imbalance is the critical first step toward holistic health. For leaders, this comprehensive approach to health is vital for enduring personal growth, effective leadership, and high performance. If you evaluate your life, considering these three dimensions of health—mind, body, and spirit—and honestly gauge your contentment on a scale from 1 (low) to 10 (high) for each aspect, how would you assess yourself?

The well-being of a leader directly influences their team. Like the nuanced relationship between a parent and child, a leader's example in maintaining their health in mind, body, and spirit becomes a template for the team. It's not about the team adopting the leader's specific practices or beliefs but being inspired to prioritize their well-being.

Leaders must recognize their profound impact on the team's collective energy. Reflect on the times when your mood—positive or negative—has set the tone for a meeting. Contrast a meeting led while you were frustrated with one where your genuine enthusiasm was palpable. The team's response often mirrors your energy, directly affecting their productivity. This underscores the importance of stress-management practices for CEOs.

The influence of a leader extends to fulfilling basic human needs: feeling seen and heard. When a leader successfully meets these needs, the team is more inclined to invest fully in the mission. To ensure your team feels acknowledged, lead by example—exemplify self-awareness and self-compassion. While this may take you out of your comfort zone, these qualities enable you to be truly present for those you guide and support.

* * *

My day begins and ends with meditation, a practice that anchors my daily routine and mitigates my stress levels. This ritual, along with leveraging the power of the breath and prioritizing sleep, underpins my approach to well-being. Mindful movement and mindful consumption are also integral to my routine. However, meditation, more than any other practice, has helped me reclaim my peace of mind, mitigating the effects of anxiety and chronic stress on my health.

I schedule my exercise, or mindful movement, in the morning, usually around 6:30, capitalizing on its stress-reducing benefits and boosting my focus and energy for the day. Aligning my exercise with the body's natural cortisol levels sets the stage for better sleep at night and boosts my metabolism throughout the day. I prefer activities like yoga and high-intensity interval training for thirty minutes four to six days a week. This duration, while shorter than what some may advise, has proven effective for my health goals while fitting into my packed schedule. My workouts are also considerate of my body's needs, allowing me to release stress intentionally and recharge my mental and physical energy without being harmful to my joints.

When considering nutrition, the timing and manner of eating are just as crucial as the food choices themselves. Keeping my digestive system robust (priming the pump) is a vital aspect of maintaining my overall health. On the dietary front, my day starts with warm lemon water for hydration, stimulating the digestive system, and alkalizing the body.

About an hour later, my daily cup of coffee has become a sacred ritual in itself.

My first meal is between 10:00 a.m. and noon, aligning with intermittent fasting practices, which improves my metabolic health by allowing my digestive system time to rest and rest. I have the most autonomy over this meal as I eat alone during a break from my work. As such, it's intentionally eaten mindfully, free from distractions (including my computer and phone), allowing me to fully appreciate the food's aroma, taste, and visual appeal. This practice of slowing down, leveraging all senses, and expressing gratitude enhances the nourishment I receive from the meal and improves digestion.

Slowing down and removing distractions during meals allows us to truly focus on our food, leading to increased awareness of hunger cues, better chewing habits, and improved digestion and nutrient absorption. Looking back, I wish I could share this understanding with my younger self, who frequently rushed through meals, often eating at my standing desk while multitasking at work, all of which can hinder our natural digestive functions.

My diet primarily consists of locally sourced, organic produce and sustainably raised meats, in line with Ayurvedic principles that encourage a balance of all six tastes. My nutrition adheres to the 80/20 rule. While it is primarily made up of fresh, unprocessed foods, it allows flexibility for indulgences. This flexibility is crucial as being too restrictive can elevate stress hormones, sabotaging our health goals.

The impact of nutrition on our ability to lead and perform efficiently is undeniable. Humans weren't designed to spend prolonged hours at a desk consuming coffee and processed foods. Despite the complexity of nutrition, at its core, it boils down to a simple truth: some foods nourish and energize us, while others don't. Opting for fresh, local, and unprocessed foods provides the body and mind with greater energy, cognition, performance, and vitality. Ultra-processed foods, on the other hand, can contribute to anxiety, obesity, and heart disease and make you feel fatigued rather than energized. Nutrition should be about nourishment, primarily focusing on energy-building foods while still enjoying variety and pleasure in eating.

Throughout the day, I take five-minute breaks to breathe and re-center, ensuring I maintain my presence and vitality. Taking just five minutes to step away from screens, ground yourself, and breathe can have several positive impacts on your health. Short breaks allow you to rest your eyes, reduce mental fatigue, and alleviate physical strain associated with prolonged screen use and chair time. More importantly, it helps lower stress levels, regulate your nervous system, and promote relaxation.

Despite a busy schedule juggling work and chauffeuring teenagers, I strive to ensure we have a wholesome dinner, even if it's later than preferred. This is where self-compassion practices become integral, recognizing that while dinner may not always be nutritionally balanced or at a normal dinner hour, the family still gets fed. The harm caused by negative thought patterns, such as self-criticism, can have a more detrimental impact on our health than the occasional nutritionally subpar meal.

To conclude the day, I have a nightly ritual to transition into rest: meditation, breathwork, journaling, and a technology detox. An evening wind-down routine free of screens is something many of us overlook, yet it is crucial for promoting quality sleep. My nightly journaling ritual is concise and purposeful, aimed at preventing racing thoughts from disrupting my sleep. It consists of three steps: jotting down any lingering concerns or challenges from the day, reflecting on three things I'm grateful for, and setting an intention for the next day. This personal routine is tailored to maintain my vibrancy, joy, and presence in daily life.

* * *

Achieving work-life balance is a deeply personal endeavor, and it varies daily. I found freedom when I let go of the idealized image of balance that society often expects of working mothers—an image that didn't align with my desires. The pivotal change came when I shifted my focus from balancing to being fully present, whether in the office or at home. This approach transformed my struggle into a fluid process.

The essence of my strategy is choosing presence over the pursuit of perfection, and meditation has been the catalyst for this transformation. My days may ebb and flow, sometimes tipping more toward work, other times toward family. Yet, each morning begins with a moment for myself—immersing in meditation to reconnect with my truth and emerge with a sense of peace.

This practice of daily meditation, grounding myself in tranquility before the day begins, is my key to managing life's demands. It equips me to handle the unexpected and lightens the burden of my responsibilities, setting a serene tone for whatever the day may bring. It also helps me show up as my most vibrant self for my team, my clients, and most importantly, my family.

* * *

Stress is an inevitable aspect of leadership roles. Mastering stress management to prevent its adverse effects on your health is essential. Chronic stress, while not a disease itself, can pave the way to illness if left unchecked. Research suggests that up to 90 percent of known diseases have connections to chronic stress. This statistic was eye-opening in my career, revealing the immense control we have over our health. With this knowledge, I decided to take charge of my well-being by choosing what intuitively feels right for my body rather than relying on the latest health trends promoted by the media.

I attribute my physical health and mental resilience to three core practices: meditation, breathwork, and mindful movement. My day begins with meditation, grounding me in my truth and inner peace.

Establishing a regular meditation practice offers dramatic health benefits. Meditation acts as a purification process, inducing deep rest. It facilitates a shift into a state of restful awareness, countering the typical fight-or-flight response prevalent during our workday. This transition results in a slower heart rate, normalized blood pressure, reduced production of stress hormones like adrenaline and cortisol, and increased production of rejuvenating hormones such as DHEA and growth hormone. Meditation slows breathing, instilling a sense of calm, and is even shown to enhance immune function.

While the physical benefits of meditation are remarkable, perhaps its most compelling aspect lies in the stillness it offers, where our inner truths are revealed. In moments of quiet reflection, solutions to lingering problems often become clear, and our intuition becomes sharper. By distancing ourselves from external influences and embracing silence, we can uncover our true selves, our authentic selves, liberated from the masks we wear to conform to societal norms and media influence. By connecting with our inner truth daily, we illuminate our confidence, significantly enhancing our capacity to lead our teams effectively.

During the day, I make it a habit to intentionally pause briefly and engage in breathwork, resetting my nervous system at the first signs of stress. Additionally, I dedicate at least five minutes every day to a breathwork practice, leveraging a variety of techniques such as the Coherent Breath. This muscle memory resulting from my daily practice, combined with deep self-awareness honed through meditation, enables me to recognize when to step back and breathe. This allows me to respond mindfully rather than mindlessly react to stressful stimuli and triggers, leading to a positive ripple effect on everyone around me.

Coherent Breathing is a straightforward technique where we aim to breathe evenly, inhaling for five to six counts and exhaling for five to six counts, resulting in about five complete breath cycles per minute. Many consider this practice to fall within the therapeutic zone of breathing, meaning it profoundly nurtures and heals our physiology. One of the primary advantages of coherent breathing is its ability to enhance heart rate variability, which refers to the variation in the time interval between heartbeats. It's a measure of the autonomic nervous system's influence on the heart and reflects the balance between the sympathetic and parasympathetic branches of the nervous system. By increasing the flexibility of the autonomic nervous system and its connection to the heart, coherent breathing promotes steadier and more resilient heart function. Research has demonstrated that coherent breathing can alleviate a range of issues, from insomnia to anxiety, both of which I have been challenged with before developing a consistent breathwork practice.

Breathwork serves as a powerful tool in leadership. I've incorporated the practice of commencing meetings with a brief grounding exercise, enabling everyone to fully present for each other and the agenda. As a leader, demonstrating this by suggesting, "The day has been hectic; let's take a moment to center ourselves before we dive in," and taking a few deep breaths yourself can both relax and focus your team (and yourself). Give it a try at your next meeting and observe how the energy in the room transforms.

Mindful movement is yet another pillar in my strategy for emotional well-being, serving as a means to release and receive. While there is much discussion on emotional intelligence in the workplace, rarely do we hear how important physical movement is to increase it.

Emotions are experienced as sensations in the body, associated with thoughts in the mind. Emotions should flow and be released after imparting their lessons; otherwise, they may manifest as physical conditions. It's estimated that two-thirds of physical ailments have emotional root causes.

I've tailored my exercise regimen to address specific emotional needs—choosing activities that foster the emotional release I require, whether that's expelling frustration with a vigorous run or fostering strength through weight training. Again, this is where meditation has been the doorway, allowing me to improve my interoceptive awareness, perceiving a subtle internal bodily sensation from within. For example, sadness can form a knot in the throat, and anxiety can feel like a tightness in the chest. Ask yourself if there is an emotion that you might be harboring physically? Exploring how your emotions influence your health can be remarkably impactful. Taking action can be as straightforward as setting the intention to process and release that emotion at the beginning of your next exercise session.

These stress-management practices of meditation, breathwork, and mindful movement are woven into the fabric of my presence-first lifestyle.

* * *

Beginning my days with meditation sets the stage for authenticity in my leadership role. It cultivates vulnerability in my approach, which, in turn, inspires my team to embrace their vulnerabilities. For instance, in a recent meeting I was facilitating, a profound sense of gratitude overwhelmed me, bringing me to the verge of tears. Instead of holding back, I allowed the emotion to surface.

Acknowledging and sharing my feelings in that moment proved to be powerful. The feedback was overwhelmingly positive, with messages of appreciation for my openness. Comments like, "Thank you for your vulnerability today; it was inspiring!" and, "You made me feel special and that you were here for us" highlighted the impact of my honesty.

This experience reaffirmed the wisdom of Brené Brown's words: "Vulnerability is the birthplace of innovation, creativity, and change." It is a cornerstone of leadership that fosters connection and transformation within a team.

* * *

Support systems are crucial for my well-being. We are inherently social beings who need connections that fulfill our emotional necessities. As one of my teachers, Deepak Chopra, emphasizes, *as humans, we have fundamental needs of attention, affection, appreciation, and acceptance.* These elements are foundational for emotional well-being. In my journey as an entrepreneur and mother, having a solid network of close, supportive friends and family has been indispensable.

Asking for support is vital, yet it requires a willingness to be vulnerable. My meditation practice has been instrumental in cultivating self-awareness, enabling me to recognize my needs, such as affection, and seek them out. Furthermore, this practice has been my backbone when my usual support system is out of reach, providing me with the foundation to provide myself the attention, affection, appreciation, and acceptance I seek. Making a point to prioritize building and nurturing your support network can improve your health. Reach out to those who uplift you and provide the emotional support you need. From a leadership standpoint, we can view our team from this perspective, utilizing the "Four A's" as a compass to nurture a culture of collaboration.

While external support systems hold significant importance, they are outweighed by the necessity of internal support systems. Achieving this internal support involves cultivating holistic health in the mind and spirit through daily habits. Crucially, these habits encompass practices such as meditation, which cultivate self-awareness and self-compassion. If you haven't yet incorporated meditation into your routine, consider it as a pivotal step forward. Remember, meditation offers a plethora of benefits with no negative side effects. It reduces stress, enhances mental health by alleviating anxiety and depression, bolsters focus and concentration, fortifies emotional resilience, and contributes to better physical health outcomes like strengthened immune function and lowered blood pressure. More importantly, meditation nurtures empathy, compassion, and patience, fostering healthier relationships with yourself and others and facilitating spiritual growth and self-discovery. In essence, it's a simple yet potent practice to build the ultimate internal support system.

* * *

The journey to holistic health encompasses recognizing the profound interconnectedness of mind, body, and spirit. It involves achieving a state of complete integration, where our physical, mental, and spiritual aspects align harmoniously. This alignment fosters a dynamic state of health characterized by vitality, resilience, and joy. As leaders, it's crucial to embody this holistic approach to health, recognizing that our well-being directly influences our team's collective energy and productivity.

By prioritizing practices such as meditation, breathwork, mindful movement, and nurturing support systems, we cultivate self-awareness, resilience, and compassion—qualities essential for effective leadership and personal growth. Embracing a presence-first lifestyle enables us to navigate the complexities of leadership with authenticity and vulnerability, fostering deeper connections and transformation within our teams. By integrating daily habits that prioritize the well-being of our mind, body, and spirit, we embody the archetype of a Fully Alive CEO—a leader who inspires others to prioritize their health and well-being.

As a Fully Alive CEO, you are a beacon of insight, guiding others toward vitality, purpose, and profound connection.

About the Author

Maria Mayes is a multifaceted professional, serving as a meditation teacher, well-being coach, and founder of Take 5, LLC, a workplace wellness company. As senior customer success manager at Kooth Digital Health, she spearheads the adoption and integration of a groundbreaking mental health app for adolescents while building community partnerships. Through Take 5 Maria integrates breathwork, meditation, and mindfulness into corporate environments, fostering wellness from the conference room to the cocktail table. Committed to enhancing the mental well-being of the collective, Maria offers 1:1 coaching to executives and leads group classes in workplaces, behavioral health facilities, and wineries. As the host of the *Chakras & Chardonnay* podcast, she brings these transformative teachings to a global audience.

Learn more at www.take5.health.

The CEO's Guide to Peak Performance Through Self-Care

Jon Hoerauf

All the skills, ambitions, and drive we have as CEOs are housed within a physical body and maintained by a human mind. If we neglect this body and mind, operating at peak performance is impossible. We tend to be dreamers and visionaries by nature, and unless we find a way to maintain this peak performance, there is no way we can achieve all our desires.

If the success of your business relied on an irreplaceable piece of equipment, you would do whatever was necessary to keep it performing at its best and avoid any unnecessary downtime. While most machines can be rebuilt or replaced, your body and mind cannot. Maintaining physical, emotional, and mental health could be one of the most important investments in your business.

Western society has evolved away from taking personal responsibility for our health to depending on drugs or surgeries to fix the symptoms that emerge from physical and nutritional neglect. It's far too common to abuse our bodies by filling them with sugar and overprocessed foods and then wonder why we have so many aches and pains. Not taking the time for exercise causes our muscles to atrophy and our stress levels to soar. Our energy levels plummet, our creativity gets muddled, and our personal and professional relationships suffer. This is a fairly recent phenomenon for us.

Years back, our ancestors ate whole foods because that was all they had. They exercised daily because they did physical work, walked rather than sat in cars, couldn't spend hours in front of the TV, and got plenty of sleep because all they had was light from lanterns. I'm not reminiscing about the good old days and saying they had it better. Their lifespans were shorter, they didn't have high-tech emergency rooms that save countless lives, and the infant mortality rate was high.

Rather than longing for a lifestyle of the past, I try to combine the best of both worlds. For instance, I remember driving my 1968 rear-wheel-drive Chevy in the winter. The windshield took forever to defrost, and I had no traction on the ice. I love the heated seats and steering wheel and all-wheel drive in my present car. However, I'm thankful I had the chance to experience doing doughnuts in the parking lot while appreciating that I no longer do them on the road.

I approach my health in the same way. I love modern society with my cell phone, laptop, and unlimited internet access. However, I want to reach back and take the best from the past. Even though it is much cheaper and easier to eat processed food, I know that spending the extra money on organic food and preparing it myself is much better for my body. Because I have a mostly sedentary job, I know it is better for me to take the time to exercise on my time off.

Anything worth doing needs to be scheduled, or it won't happen. I use a few different methods to be sure I take the time to stay healthy. The first one is out of necessity. My wife and I own two dogs that need to be walked daily because if we don't, they run around the house all evening. Even if I don't feel like walking, it's better than the alternative.

Another method I use is to schedule my workout times. I have a gym membership, and I've found that I do best when certain days are set aside to use it. Even though I enjoy working out and know it makes me feel better, I can't leave the decision to get there to my feelings each day. I have to commit to myself that I will go to the gym on certain days and run through my workout.

Finally, I take several short walks throughout the day at work. My facility has a walking path that takes about fifteen minutes to complete. Doing this two or three times a day helps me physically, clears my head, and allows me to process the project I am working on at the time.

One of the best ways to maintain emotional health is to have a clear vision. As a CEO, there are many things screaming for your attention, and it's impossible to maintain emotional well-being if you are trying to appease all of them simultaneously. A clear vision allows you to weed out the unnecessary things, reassign the less important ones, and focus on those that will take you to your goal.

Another practice I adhere to is morning quiet time. For me, this includes a cup of coffee and reading my Bible. Carving out this time, even though it means getting up early, sets the stage for the day. It calms my mind and allows me to breathe before I step into my day.

A final aspect of emotional health is practicing emotional honesty. I regularly take stock of where I am and acknowledge how I feel, whether it's angry, lonely, stressed, or something else. This allows me to stay ahead of my emotions rather than be surprised by them. Once they are acknowledged, I do my best to deal with them immediately. This may mean apologizing to someone, choosing to forgive someone, taking a few deep breaths and letting go, or a variety of other techniques that help me stay centered.

There is a dangerous time between the excitement and expectations of inspiration and the fulfillment of seeing your dream come to life. This is a time when emotional resilience is tested and stretched. It's fun to start a new project. There are hopes for changing the world. Your mind explodes with possibilities, and everything seems possible. However, at some point, the original excitement wears off, and the realization of the enormity of the project begins to set in.

Excitement can only fuel you for so long before determination needs to take over. It's during this time that emotional resilience is tested; most dreams are weeded out and left to die. The upside of this is that if you can find a way to push through, your dream will be one of the few that makes it to fruition, and since most dreams die before they see the light of day, you have less competition.

The nature of my work requires me to spend a lot of my day on my computer. This can be draining on my mind, stressful to my body, and strain my eyes. One way I deal with this is to take slow, pondering walks throughout the day. When I get stuck on a project, I take a walk. Sometimes, when I walk, I don't think of anything and allow my mind to rest. Other times, I map out my next steps in my mind from a distant vantage point, which is hard to achieve in my office while

I'm sitting at my computer. These walks allow me to see the big picture in 3D so that when I return to my desk, I can continue to focus on the details of what's next.

I also find mental clarity through stretching and practicing yoga. There is a private room where I work that's away from the day's chaos. I sometimes retreat to this room and take twenty minutes to stretch, breathe, and allow the energy of the day to flow off my body.

I intentionally work to create relationships at work during times when I don't need them, so they are there when I do. These relationships fall into various circles of trust, and I only have a couple of people in my inner circle. Of these, there is only one man at work with whom I'm totally honest. I realize that most people don't have this gift, and I know I'm fortunate for this friendship. It's refreshing and freeing to know that he won't judge me for my failures and frustrations or get competitive with me over my success. It took a long time and a lot of risks to develop this friendship, but it is worth the effort. I encourage every leader to work toward this.

On a parallel track, I work to develop a support system for my employees. I understand that if they are overly stressed or feel abandoned, they will be less productive and more prone to needing time off. I set up regular one-on-one meetings with them so we can develop a supervisory relationship based on trust and understanding. I choose to take an interest in their personal lives and care more about them than their work performance.

It's also important to create an atmosphere where your staff can develop relationships with each other. We need to balance performance with free time. There may be a need to do some team building or even an intervention within a team that is struggling. Solid work relationships create an atmosphere of trust and promote solid work performance.

We often hear the adage that the customer comes first. While I understand the intent of this viewpoint, I think it's misguided advice. The goal is to have satisfied customers who keep coming back and refer their friends. The question is, "How do we make that happen?" If we live by a customer-first approach, it often leads to ignoring or neglecting our employees. Too heavy of a focus on KPIs, customer satisfaction surveys, and performance outcomes leads to high turnover or, worse, disengaged employees who refuse to leave. Ultimately, this discord produces dissatisfied customers. I believe that if you develop healthy, satisfied employees, they will take care of their clients, and you will have the satisfied customers you desire. I aim to treat my staff the way I wish past supervisors had treated me.

I've experienced the times in life when my furnace died in the middle of the night, and I needed to wait for a repair man the next day. I've lived through days at work when it was hard to concentrate because of what I was going through in my personal life. I've messed up at work and had to sit through uncomfortable discussions with my supervisors while I listened to how disappointed they were with me.

When one of my staff sends me a text message before work stating that they are experiencing something at home, I offer as much grace as possible. When someone messes up at work, I extend the same compassion to them that I would want someone to offer me. While appointments may need to be changed and customers may experience dissatisfaction in the short term, the long-term benefits are worth it. By operating this way, I've witnessed transformations in employees that changed the course of our organization.

One example that illustrates this way of working with my staff comes to mind. One of my direct reports supervised four staff. His natural tendency was to be detailed with policies and expectations and focus most of his energy on what his staff were doing wrong. He believed that if he could stomp out their negative behaviors, they would only be left with the positive ones. This led to his staff living with anxiety about their performance and resentment toward him. With this constantly on their minds and so much of their energy going toward these feelings, they couldn't operate at their best with their clients.

One day, he was complaining to me that one of his people asked for time off for something that he thought was frivolous. He was considering "having a talk" with them. He stopped mid-sentence and commented how he appreciated that I was generous with him when he recently asked for time off at the last minute for a family event. After a moment or two of silence, he decided not to confront his employee.

A few months later, his behavior toward his staff changed, and I noticed that his team was much more comfortable in their roles and even appreciated him as their supervisor. One of his team members, who was originally very unhappy with him, told him that he needed to stay in his position at least until she was ready to go somewhere else. I also noticed that he grew to be much less defensive when he and I talked. All of this happened without me confronting him for his leadership style; I simply modeled my belief that his personal life and experience at work were more important to me than doing everything right.

I have a natural tendency to keep working without paying attention to my personal needs or the physical wear on my body. What I've noticed over time is that if I ignore my body, it tends to get my attention by getting sick. Now, when I feel that telltale discomfort in the back of my throat or lungs, I realize I need to step back for a day or two. Otherwise, I'll end up getting sick for a week.

Invest in yourself. It's easy to see our computers, buildings, and employees as investments in our business, but if you don't take care of yourself, you will burn out and get replaced like an old fax machine. It's harsh but true. If you're forty pounds overweight, smoke a pack of cigarettes a day, or work so many hours that your family feels neglected, you're headed full speed at a brick wall. It's hard to hear and even harder to find the time and motivation to change, but you only have one life. Businesses can be rebuilt. Dreams can be reimagined, but there's only one you, and you can't be replaced.

Every day, you must prioritize what to handle first and what to let go. A solid vision gives you the framework from which to make those decisions, and it's vital to include self-care in this vision. You are the only one who can fulfill your dreams; without you, those dreams will die. The most important resource you have available to ensure those dreams are accomplished is your emotional, mental, and physical health.

About the Author

Jon Hoerauf has a background as a counselor and teacher. He is a writer and professional speaker in the areas of motivation, leadership, and teamwork. To schedule him for a workshop or as a keynote speaker, you can contact him at jon@JonHoerauf.com.

How to Shift From Burnout to Brilliance: Redefining Health of Mind, Body, Spirit Through Five ALIVE Steps

Anna Choi

"The real problem of humanity is the following: We have Paleolithic emotions, medieval institutions, and godlike technology."

–Edward O. Wilson

While this conversation took place over one hundred years ago, what's changed since?

While technology's godlike powers have accelerated exponentially, our ancient, paleolithic brain impulses designed for survival have barely evolved.

We live in an age of brain overload and an attention deficit economy where the new resource extraction isn't water or air; it's our brain's attention.

How does this relate to your health as a CEO?

Due to the normalization of brain overload and high-stress hustle environments as the status quo, many high-achieving clients fail to recognize they are even in burnout.

Burnout has become a new normal until a crisis forces you to pay attention. Perhaps it's being rushed to the ER for high blood pressure, receiving an unexpected diagnosis with a life-threatening tumor or disease, or someone close passing away that has you stop and question the meaning of life.

Rather than wait for a crisis to give you a message to wake up, you can redefine what health looks like and commit to actions that will create your desired health level.

How do you define health? What is health?

I encourage you to sit with the inquiry "What is health?" rather than seeking to arrive at a conclusion. Journal what thoughts, feelings, images, memories, or visions come to mind when you think of health for you.

Looking at the dictionary, the definition of health is "the state of being free from illness or injury." It goes further, including "a person's mental or physical condition."

For CEOs, that definition hardly accounts for aging, recovering from unexpected injuries or accidents, or being able to play with your kids or grandkids.

In other words, health is being sick or injury-free. Check yourself right now. Is that what health means for you?

Are you sickness and injury-free but ten to twenty pounds overweight with high blood pressure, sugar cravings, and a sedentary lifestyle? For most, that picture, while typical, is not their definition of health.

Let's take it a step further. Suppose you are at a healthy weight and blood pressure, eat okay without binging or eating too much sugar and fats, and exercise occasionally. While that may check the box off as "good enough" for high achievers, it is still not the picture of health.

If that is a true picture of health for you, you can save yourself time and stop reading this chapter and skip to the next one.

While one could surmise this is an average "not too bad" picture of health, the kind of health I'm sharing here unleashes your full longevity potential to have a high quality of life until 120 years old.

Health redefined includes full power and energy vitality of your body, mind, heart, and soul. A total well-being of "youthing" as you age, where a stem cell scientist could take a sample of your cells and discover the cellular age of your organs is twenty years younger than your current age. This kind of healthspan is what I mean by true health.

Here are a few real-life examples of youthing seniors to inspire you:

- A ninety-six-year-old yoga instructor who began yoga for the first time in her eighties is more flexible than many children on screens all day.
- A 105-year-old cyclist wins a race, has the body of someone in their fifties, and can still touch his toes.

- A woman in her late eighties had a stroke and naturally recovered in three weeks, not from drugs but by doing yoga and qigong-based exercises and maintaining a good diet. She can drive again.

The kind of health I am talking about is possible and happening worldwide.

What if living to 120 with a high quality of life, potentially even better than when you were younger, became the norm?

Rather than shrink your life as you age to avoid injury, what if you became more boldly healthy?

I am over forty now. Yet my mind, body, heart, and soul are in far better shape than when I was overworking in my early twenties. I started taekwondo at 35 years old, became a black belt, and now train three times a week with twelve- to fourteen-year-olds. I'm able to recover from minor injuries, aches, and pains through daily qigong while making time to meditate an hour a day to be less reactive to my family and more at peace.

Physically, I still face the same aging challenges as the next person: my body is less forgiving if I miss a day of exercise. I can't do "the weekend warrior" routine of sudden intense exercise once a week and easily recover or pull an all-nighter to get something achieved. I simply don't let those limitations become reasons for letting my physical health deteriorate.

A full understanding of health goes beyond exercise, sleep, food choices, and stress levels. Health is a choice you make each moment. Whenever you choose a carrot stick instead of chocolate cake, exercise when you're tired, or stay quiet when triggered by a loved one instead of reacting with anger, your cells respond and reward you with more vitality.

Knowing what's possible for your health, it's your turn. What is your definition of health?

Take a journal out or share with someone you love what vibrant health looks like for you.

Here are some examples of holistic definitions of health:

- Complete well-being of one's mind, body, heart, and spirit
- The body's cells are in harmony
- Living to 120 with a high quality of life and health span

What is your definition of health success? Make your definition of health your own.

Now, ask yourself and journal: Where do you see the healthiest version of yourself in fifty years? Ten years? One year? Six months? Thirty days? Pick the easiest time frame for yourself to imagine.

Then, visualize in 3D, like a movie, and create vivid details of what you can imagine in your mind's eye. Who's with you? What are you doing? What do you see, taste, smell, and touch? How do you feel?

Now that you have a vision of where you want to go, let's assess your current health. Many people live in burnout without realizing it.

What is burnout?

There's no agreed-on definition for burnout due to *too many inconsistencies* in definition and assessment methods across burnout studies.

What I share on burnout is anecdotal based on my experience and what's worked best with my clients.

I'll be sharing four types of burnout from the aspect of your body, mind, heart, and spiritual well-being, along with questions for you to journal at the end of each section.

BODY: Physical Exhaustion

One day, walking into the office foyer, I collapsed from exhaustion from working sixty-plus hours per week. Still, in my mid-twenties, I realized how unsustainable my work ethic had become.

Physical burnout can creep up on us. Like a frog boiling in water, the hustle culture slowly becomes the norm you learn to power through, telling yourself, "This too shall pass." However, just because it may pass doesn't mean you have to live in it.

Meet one of my clients, Junie, who owns a health and medical insurance agency. Quarters one and three were nightmare seasons to survive every year—much like CPAs during tax season.

She'd get to the office by 7:00 a.m., drink coffee to get going, and be in back-to-back meetings for twelve hours straight. She'd drive home by 8:00 p.m., grab a glass of wine, then binge some Netflix to relax. She'd go to bed, wake up, and start the whole cycle again for days on end. She laughed at me when I asked when her next vacation was. She didn't know.

If I were to ask Junie, "Are you burned out?", she'd proudly say, as a high achiever used to this intense schedule, "No! It's just that time of year. I can handle it."

Granted, she had no hope it could look different and had to "put her head down and just get through it" for half a year. There wasn't any other option.

Junie's day-to-day snapshot is very typical of burned-out entrepreneurs and CEOs.

Your Turn

What does physical burnout look like for you? What are your warning signs or symptoms of burnout? Journal this, even if just for a minute or two. Even better if you can share this with a trusted loved one, colleague, or friend.

MIND: Mental Health Burnout

During college, I developed severe IBS, irritable bowel syndrome, from stress. Any time the phone rang, I assumed it was bad news. When I crossed the street, I imagined getting run over. If someone made a face when I walked by them, I assumed they didn't like me. My body would physiologically react to my worries, anxieties, and fears, which had me suddenly running to the bathroom many times a day.

How many of you can relate to psychosomatic challenges where your thoughts go out of control and impact you physically?

This is another face of burnout: mental health. While the stigma surrounding mental health is starting to lift, powerful CEOs boldly share their mental health challenges publicly, just like my client Joshua.

An eight-figure entrepreneur, influencer, and CEO, Daniel felt a different pressure as a CEO. He and his wife were going through the IVF process while he was dealing with a chronic blood clot in his leg that impaired his health.

"I'd gone through many coaches and programs over the years. It was hard to find the right fit to open up to and be vulnerable, addressing the many responsibilities and stress I bear," he shared.

Through simple energy practices we worked through together, Daniel shared how he now:

- Feels comfortable in his skin. He went from being self-conscious and having body dysmorphia to loving his body the way it is. He even took his shirt off in public at a beach, at peace with his body shape, which was completely out of character for him and something he hadn't done in years.

- Lost ten pounds naturally without any strict diet and exercise regime and is getting back in athletic shape, despite the blood clot in his ankle.

- Plays actively with his kids. Before, he couldn't run anymore from his ankle injury. Now, he can run in the sand with his kids and wife without thinking about his injury.

- Has more confidence. He says what needs to be said, not what he knows people want to hear, no longer trying to please others.

- Effortlessly attracts and closes huge business deals from his newfound energy and presence.

Your Turn

Write in your journal ways that mental health symptoms of burnout show up for you specifically. What do you imagine is the root cause of those symptoms? Be honest with yourself.

Share what you discover with trusted loved ones you feel safe with who actively listen without advice. Or hire a therapist or coach to guide you in the discovery process.

HEART: EMOTIONAL STRESS BURNOUT

Eventually, I sold my financial planning company and took a sabbatical to pursue my dream of being a full-time mom. Six weeks after water birthing my son Eli, I had to work long hours just to make ends meet. We were living off one income. My husband had a master's degree but was working a landscaping job digging ditches in Seattle rain, making $18 per hour.

With climbing student loans and credit card debt, we qualified for food stamps. Worst of all, we suffered in secret. My closest friends had no idea how bad it was, and I kept telling myself we'd get out of it soon enough. I was too embarrassed and prideful to admit we needed help until *four years later.*

Suffering alone in silence is endemic. It could be too much pride, like in my case, to ask for help and be vulnerable. Sometimes, it's acknowledging bigger failures or not being surrounded by supportive family and friends as you go through hard times. Loneliness or other unwanted emotions also can be a large source of stress, leading to burnout over time.

What about you? Many CEOs and business leaders face common challenges all at once, or little stressors build over a long time. Like a frog boiling in water, they don't realize how much a stressor silently impacts them until they have the space to go on a vacation or take time off. Typically, sickness strikes as the body weans off the adrenaline and cortisol that had carried it through the last intense, demanding work sprint. The body forces them to take time off from being productive. When the next cycle of work begins, the body ages faster, with less reserves and wiggle room to overwork the body.

What emotional stressors are you facing now, both in the short and long term?

Take a moment to journal them. Magic happens when a pen hits the paper; it allows your brain to process and receive downloads from a higher power versus typing or talking it out loud, so please take time to journal your stressors.

Stressor examples include taking care of aging parents and adult children, managing the pressures to perform CEO responsibilities, aging and unexpected health concerns, decision fatigue (making too many decisions each moment overloading your brain), and finding more purpose and meaning in life as mortality sets in. Perhaps you feel helpless or powerless in the face of other's suffering.

More highly sensitive people (HSP) or empathic business leaders can sense energy deeply in their bodies. Perhaps "compassion fatigue" sets in when listening to others in their family or ingesting world news, whether it's war, climate change, fires, heat waves, water shortages, or political extremism and division. Social media scrolling and the addiction to constantly checking updates and notifications drain your energy battery and steal your attention, too.

Your Turn

Please journal: What kinds of emotional stress are you currently experiencing or have you experienced recently that's weighing you down? When did you last feel hurt, rejected, embarrassed, angry, annoyed, resistant, or sad? How do suppressed emotions manifest as physical symptoms in your body?

Go ahead and set a timer for three minutes. Yes, right now in this moment. Knowing all this information won't make any difference; it just fills your brain with more noise. It's best to implement, even if it's hard to come up with anything.

Now journal: How can you shift, release, or receive support to lighten your emotional stress? Share these actions with a loved one, or hire a coach or guide to support you in implementing these new actions into your daily life.

SPIRIT: SPIRITUAL EMPTINESS BURNOUT

At sixteen, I experienced my first burnout.

On the outside, I "had it all," a solid family upbringing, good friends, and a great boyfriend. I was a scholar-athlete and award-winning violinist, and my peers elected me to be the student body vice president. However, despite these achievements, I felt empty inside. The guilt of not being happier weighed me down.

I questioned living life: "Is this it?" The emptiness inside, no matter how much money you make or what you achieve, is what I call spiritual burnout. If unaddressed, I believe it can manifest into illness or a life-threatening disease.

According to recent studies, the number one regret of those surveyed at death is not living a life true to themselves. In other words, they sold out for someone else's definition of success and health, whether their parent's, family's, or society's.

Do you know who never sells out on you? Your True Self or Soul. Pick whatever higher power name best resonates for you.

These days, burnout starts young. My parents divorced when I was fourteen, and I felt a lot of financial pressure. I was raised by a single mom, and my older sister went off to college. I had three hours of sports practice after school and kept up with college courses, going to bed after midnight and waking up early for zero hour. Running off five hours of sleep, I remember driving an hour and a half each way to my violin lessons, nodding off, and almost veering off into semi-trucks, whizzing past me at sixty miles per hour.

If you're a parent, is your kid an overachiever and already on their way to burnout? What about you? When did you first experience burnout? How old were you?

It's often tempting to want to treat the symptoms of burnout—get more sleep, cut out your commitments, etc.—rather than address the source of burnout.

This is a big pitfall. Instead, learn to ask yourself: What hole are you trying to fill inside? What are you trying to gain from your busy life and achievements? What does recognition, influence, power, more money, financial success, or impacting more people give you?

Consider this: Nothing outside yourself will ever fill that empty hole inside.

The pitfall is treating symptoms of burnout—not the source of burnout.

As mentioned earlier, there's no agreed-on definition for burnout due to *too many inconsistencies* in definition and assessment methods across burnout studies. What I share on burnout is anecdotal based on my experience and what's worked best with my clients.

What we've discovered is that the source of burnout is often a major misalignment in one's life.

Perhaps you're not being true to yourself or not living your purpose. Some people settle for a financially secure life and tell others with a fake smile, "I'm great! My life is fine; it's good," while hiding how miserable they feel inside. Some of you simply quit on your dreams. You've been burned too many times and may not even allow yourself to dream anymore because you're scared to fail again or feel rejection or heartbreak one more time. But deep down, you can't run or hide from yourself. You know that something's missing.

Your Turn
Journal where you feel empty no matter how much you achieve. What does that feel like? Name the emotion.

In what ways do you try to fill your empty voids? What kinds of healthy or unhealthy habits do you want to keep or get rid of? Where are you not being true to yourself?

NOW WHAT: SELF-ASSESS IF YOU ARE IN FLOW OR BURNOUT

Here's a quick test to determine if you're overall in flow or burnout by asking a powerful question.

In the following exercise, you may keep your eyes open or closed.

Sit back and relax in your chair. Feel your feet on the ground and your back against the seat. Take a few slow, deep breaths. Placing your hands on your heart, ask this powerful question: "If I were to pass away right now, am I ready?"

For most people, the answer is no. If that's you, ask your heart again, "What lights me up? What fills me with joy?"

Pause long enough to *feel* the response from your body. The brain may chatter an automatic response; just set that aside. Keep listening through to the other side of the silence.

You might hear a gentle whisper or a loud, jarring command. Some of you may see an image appearing in your mind's eye or an inner knowing arising. Be open to the many ways your heart's intuition communicates to you.

Then have fun and notice what gives you joy! Focus on feeling flow, the moments of brilliance where every cell in your body screams "Yes!"

Your source of burnout and brilliance is unique to you. Don't ask your loved ones or get advice from a professional. Trust the answer is within. Use your body as a compass to focus on feeling flow.

What filled me with joy was dancing and singing.

My biggest source of burnout was suppressing and denying the brightest parts of myself—the passion to sing and dance.

It took me decades to even admit these passions. *It's not practical. It's too risky and doesn't make money. It's not what a good Korean American does to create success. It's a hobby. I don't have time for a hobby. I need to make money.*

But I couldn't deny it.

As a teenager, alone at home, music was my solace when I was stressed from life. I'd crank the music up and dance my heart out full-on music-video style. I'd hear the garage door *chk chk chk.* Mom was home! I'd jump over the couch, turn the music off, and pretend I was reading.

Though my passion was a secret, it couldn't help but leak out!

By simply allowing your passion, your brilliance within can shine.

The pitfall is trying to find your passion outside yourself like it's unknown or a mystery.

Consider your passion is this big, bright, brilliant sun inside, ready to shine—if you allow it.

Consider that your passions are so natural, like the air you breathe, that you may not even notice.

Just look at your online search history. What are you curious about? What do you get obsessed about?

WHAT IF BURNOUT ISN'T BAD?

My goal in you taking the time and energy to read this chapter is that you walk away with a simple, profound shift of paradigm that allows you to effortlessly notice and take new actions aligned with your definition of health and well-being.

However, now, I'd like to flip the conversation of burnout on its head.

What if burnout isn't bad?

Consider burnout as your friend.

It's the signpost that you're off course. Like a good friend, the more you ignore burnout, the bigger warning signs it gives you to pay attention.

Most people are great at ignoring burnout's warning signs. They might drown out their burnout by binging on Netflix (just one more episode), working late into the night (oops! It's 2:00 a.m.), or just one more glass of wine (I deserve it even though my body will hate me tomorrow).

They might even drown it out with healthy habits like tracking steps, traveling to meditation retreats, or taking personal growth program after program. (*That was me!*)

These all can be valuable, except if they become the escape from facing the source of your burnout.

If you keep ignoring it, burnout will slap you in the face with a threatening disease, unknown diagnosis, or crisis you cannot ignore.

So, honor and respect burnout as your buddy checking in: "Are you sure you're on the right path here?"

KEY TO UNLEASHING YOUR BRILLIANCE

A key to unleashing your brilliance is allowing your body to relax.

A mentor of mine was a college athlete in rowing.

Curious why another team would win year after year by a long shot, he asked the team leader, "What's your secret? Do you have a special workout or take certain supplements?"

The team leader smiled and said, "No, it's what I'm not doing. See, between every row forward, I focus my energy on relaxing and recharging before the next push. That's why our team has plenty of energy to burst through the finish line and win the race."

I was struck. Who wins in life is about who can relax the best—not push the hardest.

Contrary to conventional thinking, top performance—whether as an athlete, entrepreneur, parent, teacher, or student—hinges on how well you relax.

How quickly are you able to recover and recharge between sprints of work?

What if our society's work performance metrics were based on one's ability to fully relax? *How much vacation did you take? How slow was your heart rate?*

What if our society put as much funding into mastering the art of relaxation as it did into technology apps for productivity, efficiency, and high performance?

How good are you at relaxing?

Slowing down and surrendering tend to go hand in hand with relaxation—*like best friends.*

I get it. Sometimes, life hits you hard when you least expect it. However, those most painful and dire situations are the best accelerants to discover how to relax and surrender control.

When I water-birthed my son with no drugs, after fourteen hours of early labor, my water had not broken. I risked having to go back home because I wasn't dilated enough to have the baby.

Everything I tried wasn't working. I had to surrender control.

At that moment, my body relaxed, and I went into a deep meditation. My water broke, and my body dilated from four to ten centimeters in an hour (which is unheard of). In the next hour, I water-birthed my baby boy.

Relaxing in the most painful and dire of situations accelerated the most empowering, wonderful experience of my life.

When you relax, life can flow through you.

When you relax, your brilliance shines.

Relaxing is your portal to brilliance for any passion you want to cultivate, vision you want to manifest, or dream you want to pursue.

YOU HAVE EVERYTHING YOU NEED WITHIN YOU

Your body is an instrument of brilliant energy patiently waiting for you to allow it to fully express and unleash its potential!

What you focus on will grow. To recap:

- Stop treating symptoms of burnout. Stay focused on feeling flow.
- You don't have to find your passion; just allow the passion you were born with to shine.
- Quit making burnout bad; burnout is your friend! Instead, use burnout to show you your path to brilliance. Then, relax.

If you can dare to feel what arises no matter how hard the situation is, *watch the magic unfold.*

In my songwriting journey, I used to refuse to sing solo in public and tell myself, "I have an average voice. I can't hit high notes. I have to practice hard every day, or I'll biff it on performance day.

Six months later, I premiered on a global stage at a world peace concert alongside a seven-time Emmy award winner, singing my first original song. I belted out high notes like the best without hours of practice.

The key? Relaxing.

WHY HEALTH MATTERS FOR A CEO: A SELF-ASSESSMENT

Is health a priority for you?

Be honest. For some of you, a loud, resounding yes just reverberated through your body.

For others, you've realized reading these pages that while you say health matters, your actions say otherwise. If that's you, it's not too late; now is your moment to commit to yourself. You're worth it.

Others may be in between.

Journal the following: Rate your overall energy level. Where are you on the spectrum of health, based on your unique definition, at this moment?

1. On a scale of one to ten, with ten being super full of energy and able to replenish anytime and one being super burned out, what level of energy do you have today?
2. What has been your level of burnout in the last thirty days?

3. What is your goal for the next thirty days?

Let's look at three areas most people find important to them.

4. On a scale of zero to one hundred, what percentage would you score yourself for:
   - Health of body
   - Happiness of heart
   - Peace of mind

5. Once you rate yourself, next to each percentage score, rate yourself again from zero to one hundred for the level you are responsible for that particular area. One hundred means you are 100 percent responsible for that area being fulfilled to the score you want.

For example, if you rate your health of body at 80 percent, next to that, you might rate yourself 50 percent for taking the time to do all that you know is good for your body.

Your Turn

Journal: What do you notice about your scores or ratings? Do they align with what you thought, or did they surprise you?

What would 100 percent health, 100 percent happiness, and 100 percent peace look like in your day-to-day reality?

Take the time to imagine this. How would you feel, and who are you with? Use all your senses: what do you see, hear, taste, smell, and touch? Make as vivid a movie as you can in your mind, fully feeling it.

If the feelings aren't there, again, this becomes a pointless exercise that won't work. Do your best to feel deeply whatever you imagine.

What clothes are you wearing? What are you driving? What are you eating and drinking? Where are you going? What thoughts come to mind?

The degree to which you make this movie of the future you vivid is the degree to which your happy, healthy, peaceful future vision more easily manifests.

What does your full health of mind, body, heart, and spirit look and feel like to you?

Returning to your definition of true, holistic health, let's inquire into this question.

What are moments when you are in a full flow state, where time disappears, you're happy to simply be alive, and you trust yourself 100 percent to allow the next moment to unfold?

Here's a list I created for myself and have completed to help you develop ideas. (Yes! It's possible!)

- Waking up naturally at 5:00 a.m. without an alarm, eager to greet the day
- Meditating consistently for one hour each morning
- Enjoying yoga four to five times weekly
- Fun cardio like dancing or martial arts classes five times weekly
- Plenty of leisure time to pursue hobbies like songwriting, dancing, and traveling around the world with weeks of time totally off per year
- Strong willpower around what food I put in my body that make my cells buzz with aliveness
- Feeling at home in my body

- Strong peace of mind and able to flow with than react to the unexpected
- Consistent, weekly quality-time date nights feeling intimate and in love with my life partner
- Investing and hitting financial metrics in business with ease
- Working with incredible team members who uplift one another
- Passive income filling my bank accounts while I sleep
- Feeling in love with myself for no reason
- Experiencing bliss, inner peace, joy, and aliveness at will at any moment, no matter what is happening in life
- Welcoming into my heart any fears, triggers, or challenges with grace
- Trusting my wisdom within to guide me through uncertainty
- Being part of generative communities that help me be a better human
- My lifestyle is an ongoing meditation retreat experience to experience boundless brilliance within
- Gratitude pours through my body, and I regularly break down crying tears of joy for being alive on this planet Earth for no reason other than simply being alive

How good are you willing to have it?

Many of my clients are most confronted by creating new living visions for themselves beyond the basics, but this is where the fun part sets in.

Use the list above to inspire your snapshots of what life in full health and well-being looks like from the perspective of your mind, body, heart, and soul.

Your Turn

Take a moment to meditate and visualize your best self. Looking back at whatever memories come to mind, when were you happiest? What are your greatest moments of joy, where you were fully energized and lit up—where every cell in your body was alive and screaming *Yes!*

Open your eyes and journal all those experiences.

Now, what were the common feelings in those memories? Feel them now.

Keeping those feelings and memories, close your eyes again or keep them open. Visualize floating your body into a future you and experiencing all those feelings of happiness and great moments of joy. You can pick any timeframe—tomorrow, one year from now, or ten years in the future, whatever resonates with you.

Trust your unconscious to do the work. The less you think, the better. Just keep focusing on the feeling.

Now, *feel* into that future memory (as if it's already happened) a scene of you being in full vitality, health, and aliveness with all those moments of joy and happiness. Once you feel it again in that future memory, here are questions to ask yourself:

- How do you feel in your heart? In your body? In your mind? In your soul?
- Who are you surrounding yourself with at work and in your family? What culture are you creating?
- What do you see yourself doing first thing each morning? Feel in your body what that's like.
- What replenishes you? What habits have you developed? What is your health like?

- In this world of becoming your most brilliant self, what energy levels are you experiencing at the end of the day?
- What continues to grow in and around you?
- What do your family relationships look, feel, sound, or smell like? With your partner, kids, parents, and friends?
- Imagine hardship or challenges arising in this state. What do you do? How do you respond?

Now, open your eyes and journal everything you saw, heard, felt, and anything else you'd like to jot down.

If not much came to mind, below are health memories or scenes you can use for ideas:

- *You feel calm and grounded no matter what unexpected life thing happens.*
- *You can be with triggers more powerfully.*
- *Instead of reacting, you can pause and breathe more easily.*
- *Your brain has room to create after work and engage in your passion.*
- *You feel fulfilled in life and say out loud, "I am so blessed! I cannot believe how wonderful my life is! I'm so grateful."*
- *You're overcome with tears of joy for no reason and must stop and allow yourself to sob with the feeling of aliveness.*
- *You love your family more deeply.*
- *You're in love with you with all your mistakes, failures, and messiness.*
- *You enjoy being alone and/or in silence to connect with your spirit.*

- *You have delightful "out of this world" energy, and phenomena and synchronicities randomly occur.*
- *You quickly manifest your desires, visions, and dreams—sometimes in minutes!*
- *You feel so much pleasure being in flow.*
- *You feel so grateful for being alive.*
- *You thank triggers, hardships, and the "shit" in life at the moment as the access and opportunity for growth in that moment.*
- *You feel profound acceptance for yourself and all of life.*

Feeling this vision of brilliance, look at where you are now. Accept the current reality of the now. Notice the gap.

Now, let's get into action in that space between this vision and your self-assessment. Below are five ALIVE principles you can use as a step-by-step guide in your journey to brilliance, health, and vitality.

FIVE ALIVE PRINCIPLES

ALIVE is an acronym for the five principles: Allowing Yin to Yang, Listening Within, Inspiring Soul First, Valuing Fears, and Energizing Daily Flow. These principles have been distilled over several years from life experience, rigorous personal practice, tracking results, and many student experiences from my group coaching programs to ensure they work and are durable through change and transition.

I'm happy to say that through one of the biggest global upheavals—the COVID-19 pandemic—these ALIVE principles supported ALIVE students' minds, bodies, hearts, and souls before, during, and after through many challenging situations.

ALIVE got massively stress-tested (no pun intended). The degree to which you practice and integrate these principles in daily life is the degree to which you'll have more powerful effects.

You can learn more about each ALIVE principle and how to apply them if you visit soljoy.life/ALIVE365 or scan the QR code listed at the end of this chapter. I'll now share a high-level overview of each principle and its powerful impact when applied.

ALLOWING YIN TO YANG

In the entrepreneur world, an imbalance and "yang energy" culture pushes for nonstop growth at all costs, normalizing an unsustainable hustle and grind that is the antithesis of health. The anecdote? Adding more yin to yang energy (or vice versa), depending on what's more out of balance.

Typically, high achievers on the verge of burnout will benefit from adding more "yin energy" actions in the realm of resting, relaxing, recharging, and receiving. This requires strengthening your ability to sense energy within your body so you are aware of what needs more replenishing inside.

For those who have too much yin energy (you are in depression, recovering from trauma, or prone to inaction or lethargy), then integrating more yang energy will be required.

Both energies are valuable, but when out of balance, either extreme becomes detrimental to our health. For high-achieving entrepreneurs, especially in the Western world, I mostly focus on adding more yin energy since the imbalances with my clients mostly involve too much yang energy.

Allowing Yin to Yang helps you:

- Plan and integrate intentional restorative yin time like nature into your daily, weekly, monthly, quarterly, and annual flow of rhythms.
- Build support structures so you feel more time freedom than constant pressure from unending, often self-imposed deadlines.
- Sustain self-care, creating environments that prioritize well-being first.

LISTENING WITHIN

There's a lot of noise in the world. From deep fakes by AI to negative news, to your kid asking the same question repeatedly, or too many email newsletters and app notifications to handle single-handedly, your attention span or "mindshare" is what many big tech, social media, or advertising companies want their hands on.

It is said that we receive more information in a day than someone used to in their entire lifetime. While this remains to be proven from a credible source, we didn't always have so many choices at the grocery store or customized colors to pick from when buying things online.

Your time and attention are precious. Where your mind goes, energy flows. So, the question is: how do you pierce through all that noise to listen within?

Once you choose to listen within, another noise arises from your thoughts, emotions, body sensations, future worries, and memories. Not to mention the trauma you may carry that you don't even realize is within your cells. How do you navigate the "inner committee" of your mind? How do you feel what your heart wants?

Listening Within allows you to:

- Make clear decisions based on love than fear that expand your true self.
- Practice following your intuition.
- Clear the noise within learning how to allow, accept, and purify your thoughts, feelings, and body sensations

INSPIRING SOUL FIRST

While many high achievers have a morning ritual, it's often not conscious. For example, they might listen to the news while exercising on the treadmill rather than tune into their own body sensations and breathe in the moment. Or perhaps they watch a funny video over breakfast that fills their brain with information than being more present in chewing their food slowly and feeling grateful. In short, your mind goes outside the body, not inside to connect with your heart and be present.

Inspiring Soul First is about prioritizing deepening your connection with the soul by creating micro habits that ignite the light of your Soul. So, beyond a healthy morning routine, it's about consciously connecting to your heart while you do or do not do an activity first thing upon waking up, through your day, and before bed.

Inspiring Soul First allows you to:

- Connect more deeply with your soul through daily habits that nurture you first thing upon waking up or before going to bed.

- Discover what grounds you for the rest of your day in tiny micro habits.
- Energetically replenish yourself throughout the day to finish with more energy by the end of the day.

VALUING FEARS

It's not about conquering your fears but shifting your relationship to fears by noticing, observing, and allowing the body sensations and thoughts that come with fears to simply be.

This principle treats fears like children you can nestle under your arms instead of threatening monsters to survive, escape, or attack. It's learning how to stay nonreactive when triggered and daring to feel the body sensations of an unwanted emotion that may arise with a fear. Eventually, with practice, you can feel genuinely grateful for the fear in surfacing whatever lesson or trauma your true self is ready for to return to who you really are.

Valuing Fears allows you to:

- Intuitively experience fear and pain as a body-sensation energy you have a choice to allow to flow through you in the moment or not.
- Observe and appreciate fears for the lessons they teach.
- Flow and channel fears through your body in a healthy way as an access to growth and enlightenment.

ENERGIZING DAILY FLOW

Many high-achieving entrepreneurs think and sit too much. All day, their bodies don't move enough to circulate their energy, causing soreness, stiffness, pain, and proneness to injury if they attempt to be a weekend warrior, doing a sudden intensity of exercise too much too fast.

Energizing daily flow is about mastering the art of movement and living the ancient principle of "water up, fire down." Often, our brains are too overloaded with distractions, decision fatigue, and stress, resulting in a hot, reactive brain. Meanwhile, the energy in our guts is often stagnant from many humans eating poorly, sitting too much in a bad posture, and staring at a screen too many hours a day.

The "Water Up, Fire Down" principle is an eastern-based philosophy coined by Ilchi Lee that is anecdotal and has been studied for thousands of years by energy masters on creating a balanced energy circulation.

We often have hot heads from thinking a lot (fire energy), while our guts are stiff and cold (water energy). Bringing the fire energy in your head down to your core and bringing cool water energy up to have a calm, cool head allows for proper energy flow and circulation.

Your lower abdomen, or Dahnjon (Korean for energy center), is the battery center of the body. Once activated, it can power up and revitalize your organs and meridian channels (energy pathways in the body), deepen your breathing, and boost your immune system to prevent insomnia, high blood pressure, headaches, and many other physical or emotional pains.

Energizing Daily Flow allows you to:

- Fire up the belly and calm the mind through the ancient Tao principle "Water Up, Fire Down," which revitalizes and refuels your inner life-force energy.

- Practice simple exercises to move your body throughout the day
- Strengthen the mind-body connection to be more present and at peace to take positive actions more easily in your day.

THREE PRACTICES TO SHIFT INTO BRILLIANCE

1. Feeling an Energy Ball

Energy comes in the form of light, sound, and vibration. Energy comprises the building blocks of all matter, from the stars to the oceans and mountains, to your body, to microscopic atoms invisible to the naked eye. Energy also includes your thoughts, feelings, and body sensations.

Let's experience how energy feels.

Shake your hands like you're screwing a light bulb in. Great! Now, clap ten times. Rub your hands together to create friction and heat. Now, slap your hands up and down.

Pause and feel the sensation of your hands. Do you feel a tingly sensation or heat or magnetic sense? That's energy.

Imagine a big, bright energy ball between your hands. Focus your awareness on the space between your hands. Where your mind goes, energy flows. Don't forget to breathe.

As you inhale, expand your energy ball bigger; as you exhale, contract the ball. Imagine the ball growing brighter. Inhale and exhale. Take a last big inhale, and bring the energy ball into your heart on the exhale. Imagine and feel that energy permeating the rest of your body.

Now, ask your heart: What is my message today?

Listen within. Whatever message you get is perfect. You can now open your eyes.

Let that message ground you for your day despite any chaos.

You can give that energy ball anywhere—your brain, core, or to someone else.

You can ask yourself, "What's my message for today?" not just to your heart; you can ask any organ or pain and listen within to generate peace anytime in any chaos.

2. **Releasing Energy Blocks in the Body Using Three NOW Steps**

Now, let's directly practice allowing chaos by facing unwanted emotions or physical pain using a method introduced to me by a mind-body coach and former Stanford neuroscience researcher, Uma Sangvhi.

Ready?

I invite you to close your eyes and scan your body from your head to your toes.

1. Where do you notice tension, pain, or unwanted emotions?
2. Ask yourself: Where is that pain located? What color? What shape? What texture? What movement?
3. Now, go to another part of your body that feels good or neutral, or you can imagine one of your happiest memories. How does it feel? Warm and tingly?
4. Saturate every cell in your body with the energy of that feeling.

5. Now, go back to the pain. Ask yourself: What color is the pain? What shape? What texture? What movement?

6. Repeat this exercise, going between what feels good in your body, letting that feeling wash through your body, noticing your fear or pain, and observing its shape, texture, and movement.

Now, you can open your eyes.

When I do this exercise with clients, many people experience the shape or color shifting, sometimes disappearing altogether. Some can even transmute the painful body sensation or unwanted emotion into a healing energy.

The result of getting rid of that energy is less important than your ability to practice observing or watching your fears rather than react to them.

Don't focus on the result. Focus on simply being with what is.

3. Moving Meditation

This is based on the work of energy master Ilchi Lee. He met with the UN Ambassador of El Salvador, a small Central American nation plagued by civil war, poverty, and gang violence.

Ilchi Lee took that training into schools, training teachers to share these somatic moving meditations with their students. There was such success in kids creating peace in extremely chaotic situations that it spread to other schools. Seven years later, one in four schools from El Salvador's entire education system uses these simple mind-body-moving meditations.

Inspired, I created a local scholarship fund through our local Kitsap Community Foundation, providing training to teachers to lead these mind-body somatic exercises in class with students.

Imagine our next generation of leaders learning to access peace in chaos, transforming communities one school at a time.

Let's experience a couple of one-minute moving meditations now.

1. Pinky Thumb Exercise: Hold out both hands as fists, knuckles facing out. Take out your thumb, pointing outside on the one hand and pinky on the other hand. Now switch. Your brain's right and left lobes are integrating, relaxing your brain and helping you focus. This is a favorite for kids before taking tests and can be used anytime you face chaos.

2. Intestinals: Now, we're going to exercise our intestines! We often exercise our muscles, but how often do we exercise our organs? Place both thumbs on your belly button, palms flat on your belly, just resting. Then suck your belly button toward your spine like a sit-up crunch. Breathe normally.

You can do this in a check-out line, driving, or sitting at your desk anytime. Can you feel the heat?

Great work. Now, you can rest.

Moving meditations throughout your day bring your awareness from outside yourself into your body to generate peace in the chaos.

Your body will feel more light, warm, and grounded. You can view video trainings on intestinals and other exercises at www.soljoy.life/freetraining.

You've Got This

Remember Junie from the beginning of this chapter? After applying the exercises and ALIVE steps, she created a new level of health and well-being like never before. Her vision of health became a reality. If she can do it, you can, too.

Instead of expecting burnout and powering through it, Junie scheduled her first vacation. She created a custom schedule where she'd sleep in on certain days and now trusts her team to take more on. This allowed her space to replenish her energy. She joined a choir, created group walks with girlfriends in the morning, and had time for hobbies like thrift shopping during her busiest business seasons. Bye-bye burnout!

She shared this story with me of how she was walking down her foyer into the lobby, when a competitor colleague asked, "Are you still in business?"

Junie was confused but replied, "Yes."

"But how can you have time to hang posters for your choir during our busiest season?"

All she could say was, "My coach!"

During her hardest business quarter, Junie shifted from burnout and is now living her brilliance. Imagine if you could, too.

Health is Wealth

"Consider wealth is what's left after you've lost everything."

–Roger James Hamilton

If you consider health is wealth, imagine all your wealth is gone. What level of health are you left with to live the rest of your life?

You can create a new normal of healthy, vibrant cultures and communities by transforming your health into unimaginable heights. Committing to higher health starting today will cause a ripple effect on those around you, inspiring them to live a life of more vitality and aliveness. You can set up a brighter future of "youthing" as you age in cellular harmony.

It's never too late to start. Start by taking one tiny step, then find a community. Find a trusted friend who will push you or hire a professional to ensure you take new yin actions consistently over time.

The most important key is creating consistent, healthy habits. Track your progress. You can only manage what's measured.

The second most important key for sustainable success is creating a fertile environment of support to help you stay on track and develop consistent healthy habits for the long haul.

Don't share your health vision and goals with people who won't understand or nay-say you. It is very important to allow your seed to germinate until its roots are strong enough to withstand the elements of those who don't think what you want is possible.

Get support from a trusted health, wellness, or well-being coach aligned with your values who holds you accountable to your health vision while being there to lift you up if you feel down. Or find a friend who will call you out when you resist. Just be realistic with finding the right person to be by your side in creating a new healthier you.

As humans, before our precious time on planet Earth passes, each moment, we have an opportunity to shine our light as bright as possible, unleashing our brilliance.

May you shine your light as bright as possible, embodying your fullest expression of health.

RESOURCES

For all the resources mentioned in this chapter, visit soljoy.life/ALIVE365 or scan the QR code below

About the Author

Anna Choi, Founder & CEO of Soljoy, 2x TEDx Speaker, Performance Artist, Energy Master, & Black Belt trains high achieving leaders to shift from scattered overwhelm to a relaxed presence tapping into boundless energy so they feel more health, happiness, and peace.

Trained by two enlightened energy masters, Ilchi Lee and H.H. Sai Maa, Anna distills ancient wisdom into modern day somatic mindfulness and sound healing practices serving thousands of students to embody their soul's joy, elevating humanity's consciousness.

Her proudest accomplishment is water birthing her son Eli. She's celebrating 21 years with her sweetheart Leo, living in Poulsbo, WA with their cat Max. Learn more at https://soljoy.life and contact Anna here: https://linktr.ee/annasunchoi

THE CEO'S JOURNEY TO
HOLISTIC HEALTH

DR. DAVID YODER

I've come to understand that health isn't just about the absence of illness. It's a dynamic balance between my mind, body, and spirit, each aspect contributing to my overall well-being. Imagine health as a form of energy, a force that propels me forward, allowing me to embrace life's vast experiences and challenges with vigor and enthusiasm.

Mental energy plays a crucial role in this balance. It's the power behind my thoughts, emotions, and perceptions. When my mind is in a good place, I find clarity and focus, making it easier to solve problems and make decisions. It's like having a clear map and a bright light guiding my journey, ensuring I don't stumble in the darkness of confusion or indecision.

On the other hand, physical energy is the foundation of my ability to act in the world. It gets me out of bed in the morning, ready to tackle the day's tasks. Whether pursuing my career goals, engaging in hobbies, or simply enjoying a walk in the park, my physical well-being determines how much I can do and how well I can do it. It's the fuel that powers my body's engine, driving me toward my aspirations with strength and endurance.

Spiritual energy, though less tangible, is equally vital. This deep, inner force connects me to something greater than myself, providing a sense of purpose and direction. This energy nurtures my soul, offering comfort in times of trouble and inspiration when searching for meaning. It's a guiding star, leading me to live a life aligned with my values and beliefs, fostering a sense of peace and fulfillment.

When these three energies are high and in harmony, life truly becomes a richer experience. I'm not just surviving; I'm thriving, capable of giving my best to my career and making meaningful contributions to my community. It's a state where I can fully engage with the world around me, offering my talents and efforts to make a positive impact.

Achieving this synergy is an ongoing process, a journey of self-discovery and mindful living. It requires attention and care, making choices that nurture my mind, body, and spirit. By striving for this balance, I open myself to living life to its fullest potential, embracing every moment with passion and purpose.

When I first encountered Dr. Stephen Covey's *The 7 Habits of Highly Effective People*, it was as if a new door opened in my understanding of personal development. Among the powerful principles he shares, the seventh, "Sharpen the Saw," deeply resonated with me. This idea, simple yet profound, advocates for the necessity of self-renewal and care to enhance our effectiveness in every aspect of life.

"Sharpen the Saw" speaks to the essence of sustaining oneself, drawing a vivid picture of what happens when we neglect our maintenance. Just like a saw that becomes dull with constant use, our minds, bodies, and spirits also wear down when we push ourselves relentlessly without pause. Covey's analogy struck a chord with me, highlighting a truth often overlooked in our hustle culture: continuous effort without rest leads not to greater achievement but to burnout and diminished productivity.

This principle reminds me of the biblical narrative where even God rested on the seventh day after creating the world. If the Creator observes such a powerful act of resting, it underscores the universal need for rest and renewal across all creation, including humans. This rest isn't about laziness or shirking responsibilities; rather, it's a strategic pause, a deliberate act of self-care to recharge our batteries so we can return to our tasks with renewed vigor and sharper focus.

In practice, "Sharpen the Saw" has become my guiding philosophy. It means taking time out for myself, not as a luxury but as a necessity for maintaining my effectiveness in work and life. This encompasses caring for my physical health through exercise and proper nutrition, nurturing my mental well-being with reading and learning, tending to my emotional health through connections with loved ones, and fostering my spiritual wellness through meditation and reflection.

By adopting these habits, I've noticed a significant difference in how I approach my work and interact with others. Instead of being one among many who are constantly "on," pushing themselves to the brink of exhaustion, I choose to step back regularly. This approach has not only increased my productivity but has also improved my creativity and problem-solving abilities. I return to my tasks with a clear mind and a stronger sense of purpose, often outperforming those who never took a break.

In embracing the wisdom of "Sharpen the Saw," I've learned that true effectiveness is not measured by how much we can accomplish without stopping but by how we can sustain our pace with intentional breaks. It's a lesson in the art of balance, teaching us that by taking care of ourselves, we are better equipped to face the challenges of our work and make meaningful contributions to the world around us.

My days don't just begin when the sun rises; they're set into motion the night before. Understanding the power of restorative sleep, I've made it a ritual to retire early, distancing myself from the harsh glow of screens that could disrupt my body's natural rhythms. Nestled into my bed, the grounding mat beneath me serves as a silent healer, diminishing inflammation and restoring my body's equilibrium as I sleep.

Upon the break of dawn, my first act is not to reach for my phone or to be swallowed by the urgency of the day's tasks. Instead, I greet the morning with a glass of Sole water, a simple yet profound concoction of water saturated with Himalayan salt. I've found this balances my hydration and mineral levels, setting a tone of wellness for the day. My stretching routine follows, an essential prelude that awakens my muscles and joints, preparing them for the day's exertions.

The highlight of my morning is a rigorous tennis session lasting ninety minutes. This isn't merely a sport to me but a vital component of my wellness regimen. It challenges me physically and mentally, serving as a high-intensity workout that sharpens my reflexes and fortifies my endurance. Following this, I replenish my body with proteins and carbohydrates, mindful of the fuel I provide to recover and sustain the energy levels I require for the day.

With my physical well-being tended to, I focus on my schedule, reviewing the list of clients I will meet. This act of preparation ensures I can navigate my workday with ease, allowing me to focus fully on each interaction without the distraction of logistical concerns.

But my morning routine isn't solely about physical preparation. As I journey to work, I cultivate a practice of gratitude, reflecting on the aspects of my life that bring me joy and fulfillment. This practice grounds me, offering perspective and a profound sense of contentment that I carry throughout my day.

Looking forward to serving others, I carry with me the intention to fulfill my professional responsibilities and make a meaningful impact in the lives of those I encounter. This mindset transforms each interaction, no matter how small, into an opportunity to contribute positively, reinforcing my belief in the value of service and the potential for each day to offer moments of significance and connection.

Thus, my day, which began the night before, unfolds not as a series of tasks to be completed but as a carefully curated experience, reflecting my commitment to wellness, preparedness, and gratitude. This approach enhances my effectiveness and enriches my sense of fulfillment, reminding me daily of the interconnectedness of health, purpose, and service.

Each morning, I carve out a sanctuary of time solely for myself, setting the stage for the day that lies ahead. This personal ritual, a trilogy of physical exertion, nourishment, and meditation, is not just a routine but a foundation upon which I build my day's strength and resilience. My morning workout acts as a vigorous handshake with the day, waking my body and mind with intensity and purpose. Following this, breakfast isn't merely a meal; it's an act of fueling my body thoughtfully, choosing foods that sustain my energy and focus. Meditation then serves as a quiet interlude, a moment of stillness in which I center my thoughts and intentions, preparing myself mentally for the challenges and opportunities that await.

This commitment to self-care in the morning isn't a luxury but a necessity. It equips me with the vigor to tackle the day with enthusiasm and determination. The benefits of this regimen extend beyond the personal; they influence my professional life profoundly. By dedicating the early hours to my well-being, I ensure that I approach my work with a sharp mind and a spirited heart, ready to meet the needs of my clients with patience, creativity, and empathy.

Midday, I honor this same philosophy by allowing myself a substantial lunch break. This pause is more than a chance to eat; it's an opportunity to digest physically and mentally. It's a time to step back, recalibrate, and refocus. In these moments of quietude, I often find clarity and resolve, returning to my tasks with renewed insight and energy. This break acts as a bridge between the halves of the day, ensuring that my afternoon is as productive and fulfilling as the morning.

I've discovered that the more I invest in myself through these acts of self-care, the more I have to offer to others. It's a paradox that by prioritizing my health and well-being, I enhance my ability to serve my clients effectively. This isn't selfishness; it's a strategic form of generosity. By being at my best, I can give my best, ensuring that those who rely on my expertise and support receive nothing less than my full attention, compassion, and skill.

Thus, my daily self-care practices are not merely routines; they are my commitment to excellence, both for myself and those I serve. In nurturing my well-being, I cultivate the capacity to contribute meaningfully to the lives of my clients, embodying the principle that to give fully, one must first be fully present and care for oneself.

Every day, I consciously choose to wear an attitude of gratitude like a cloak, wrapping myself in a deep sense of appreciation for life, my family, my friends, and my job. This mindset isn't just a passive feeling but a proactive approach to life, anchoring me in the present and imbuing me with a calmness that can weather any storm. It's as if by focusing on what I have rather than what I lack, I'm able to see the world not as a series of obstacles but as a place brimming with opportunities and blessings.

In my journey, I've also discovered the power of biohacking, or small, science-backed adjustments to my lifestyle, designed to enhance my body's ability to handle stress and unexpected challenges—those curve balls life sometimes throws at us. Among the myriad of strategies available, one stands out to me as particularly effective: nurturing a strong vagus nerve to boost heart rate variability (HRV).

The vagus nerve is like a communication superhighway between the brain and the body, playing a critical role in regulating our stress response. High heart rate variability, a measure of the variation in time between each heartbeat, indicates a balanced autonomic nervous system and, by extension, a body well-equipped to deal with stress. It means that my body can shift seamlessly from a state of alertness to relaxation, maintaining a balance crucial for emotional and physical health.

To strengthen my vagus nerve and improve my HRV, I've incorporated practices such as deep, slow breathing, meditation, and regular physical activity into my daily routine. These activities don't just help at the moment; they rewire my body's response to stress over time, building a foundation of resilience that allows me to face life's ups and downs with equanimity.

Moreover, this focus on maintaining a strong vagus nerve and high HRV has taught me a valuable lesson about resilience and emotional health: It's not about avoiding stress or eliminating challenges but about cultivating an inner strength that allows me to navigate them with grace and flexibility. This approach has transformed how I experience life's inevitable stresses, not as threats but as opportunities to grow stronger and more adaptable.

In combining an attitude of gratitude with biohacking, I've found a powerful formula for staying present, calm, and resilient in the face of life's uncertainties. It's a reminder that our greatest tools for navigating life are often found within ourselves, waiting to be nurtured and developed. Through this practice, I'm not just surviving; I'm thriving, fully engaged with the present, and ready to embrace whatever comes my way with open arms and a steady heart.

In the world of healthcare, where the lines between life and death blur daily, I find myself constantly navigating emotional terrain that tests the very limits of my resilience. Each day brings with it a reminder of the fragility of human life and the weight of responsibility resting on my shoulders. It's a profession that demands not just technical skill but the deep emotional strength that's been both my challenge and my teacher.

Learning to view each experience not as a measure of success or failure but as an opportunity for growth has been a transformational shift in perspective for me. This mindset doesn't diminish the gravity of losing a patient; such moments are profoundly emotional and indelibly mark the soul. Yet, within this heartache, I've found a profound lesson about the essence of my role. It's a realization that my duty isn't to forestall the inevitable departure that comes with death but to enrich the journey toward it, ensuring it's as full and meaningful as possible for those under my care.

This understanding has gently guided me to embrace the concept of "heart memories," those intangible yet profoundly felt moments that linger in the heart long after someone's passing. Each patient I've cared for, each life that has slipped through my fingers, has left an imprint on my heart, teaching me about the depth of human strength, the resilience of the human spirit, and the boundless capacity for love and compassion we carry within us.

These heart memories are not just remnants of loss and sorrow; they are beacons of learning, guiding me to live my life to the fullest. They remind me daily of the importance of presence, of making each moment count, not just in my professional life but in every aspect of my being. They've taught me to cherish the connections I make and to approach each day with a heart open to learning and a soul ready to embrace whatever comes with grace and courage.

In this journey, I've learned that emotional resilience in healthcare is not about shielding oneself from life's pain or inevitable outcomes. It's about learning to navigate these experiences with grace, allowing them to teach us, shape us, and, ultimately, guide us to a deeper understanding of life itself. It's about carrying forward the heart memories we gather along the way, letting them illuminate our path to the next chapter with wisdom, compassion, and an unyielding appreciation for the preciousness of every moment we are given.

Navigating the complexities of mental health has been a journey of discovery and dedication for me. My approach is holistic, intertwining various physical and emotional wellness aspects to create a balanced state of being. My practice focuses on the vagus nerve, a critical element in our body's ability to manage stress and maintain inner equilibrium. I use a specialized device designed to stimulate this nerve, enhancing its function and, by extension, my overall sense of calm and well-being.

My strategy doesn't stop there. I've learned that mental health is not sustained by a single action or habit but by a symphony of them. Nutrition plays a vital role; I'm mindful of what I consume, ensuring my diet supports my physical health and mental clarity. Exercise, too, is a cornerstone of my routine, a physical manifestation of working through stress and building resilience.

Sleep and sunlight are my daily rituals, non-negotiable elements that feed my soul as much as my body. Quality sleep is the foundation upon which I build my day, while sunlight is my connection to the natural world, a reminder of the cycles and rhythms outside my experience.

Yet, perhaps the most fulfilling aspect of my approach to mental health is my commitment to service. Helping others enriches their lives and brings me a profound sense of purpose and joy. It's a tangible expression of love and compassion, a way to step outside myself and contribute to the greater good.

In striving to stay heart-centered rather than head-centered, I've discovered a path more about being than doing. It's a perspective that values empathy, intuition, and emotional connection, guiding my interactions with others and shaping my approach to wellness.

Leading by example, I've dedicated nearly three decades to researching and practicing the principles of health and well-being. Now, as I guide my clients on their journeys back to health, I draw on both my professional expertise and personal experience. It's a responsibility I don't take lightly, understanding that the path to wellness is as much about the mind and spirit as it is about the body.

My approach to mental health is a testament to the belief that we are complex beings, requiring a multifaceted approach to truly thrive. In combining science with soul, I've transformed my life and have been given the privilege to assist others in doing the same, guiding them to a place of health, balance, and profound well-being.

The year 2019 marked the onset of a period in my life that tested every ounce of my personal and professional resilience. It was a year that brought with it a storm that I navigated with determination, fueled by my love for my wife and a commitment to my practice. My wife's diagnosis of breast cancer came as a devastating blow, a moment that reshaped our lives in ways we couldn't have imagined. The challenge was magnified by the emergence of the COVID-19 pandemic, which imposed restrictions that felt like barriers between my wife and the support she needed. The inability to be by her side, to hold her hand through chemotherapy treatments, was a source of profound helplessness and sorrow.

As my personal life was engulfed in uncertainty, my professional world also came to an abrupt pause. The pandemic forced my practice to a halt, as patients were advised to stay home, leaving me in a state of professional limbo. In this moment of stillness, however, I found a new direction—a purpose that demanded my focus and energy.

Determined not to be paralyzed by the situation, I channeled my efforts into extensive research on holistic cancer treatments and recovery methods. I dove into medical journals, spoke with experts, and explored every credible source that could offer a glimmer of hope. My mission was clear: to arm myself with the knowledge that could support my wife's battle against cancer and offer solace in the face of this daunting journey.

Simultaneously, I turned to expanding my professional network, recognizing the potential of LinkedIn as a tool not just for career advancement but as a lifeline in this critical time. My network grew from about 1,500 followers to an impressive 5,000, each connection representing a potential ally in my quest for knowledge. This community became invaluable, offering insights into natural cancer cures and COVID-19 treatments that complemented conventional medicine. The information and support I received were instrumental in navigating the complexities of my wife's illness and the pandemic's impact on my patients' health.

The outcome of this concerted effort was nothing short of miraculous. My wife made a full recovery, a testament to the power of love, science, and the collective wisdom of a community willing to share their knowledge and support. Similarly, the strategies I learned through my research and networking significantly bolstered my patients' immune systems, providing them with the resilience needed to face the pandemic.

This challenging chapter of my life underscored the importance of adaptability, resilience, and the strength of community. It taught me that even in the face of overwhelming odds, a combination of love, relentless pursuit of knowledge, and the support of a like-minded community can lead to extraordinary outcomes. My wife's recovery and the positive impact on my patients stand as a testament to this belief, serving as a beacon of hope and a reminder of the power we hold when we come together to face life's most daunting challenges.

The transformation in my approach to healthcare, from reacting to crises to emphasizing prevention and ongoing maintenance, has significantly altered the lives of my clients. This shift in perspective alleviates immediate discomfort and fosters a deeper, more sustainable form of well-being. One particular story stands as a testament to this approach's effectiveness.

I recall a client who, driven by the pressures of a demanding job and the tumult of life, would seek my assistance only when his health issues had escalated to the point of severe pain and distress. Each visit was a desperate attempt to quell the storm that raged within his body, a cycle of relief followed by neglect until the next inevitable crisis.

Our breakthrough came when we managed to stem one such episode of acute discomfort. During this period of calm, we engaged in a candid discussion about the nature of stress and the relentless demands of his professional life. Together, we acknowledged that while certain external pressures were beyond our control, we had the power to change how we responded to them.

The solution we arrived at was a maintenance program, a proactive and consistent approach to his health that would serve as a buffer against the stressors of his life. This wasn't merely about scheduling regular appointments; it was about fostering a new mindset that viewed health as a priority rather than an afterthought.

The impact of this shift was profound. Not only did my client begin to enjoy our regular sessions, viewing them as an integral part of his life, but the benefits also extended far beyond the confines of my practice. He reported a significant salary increase directly due to his improved productivity and presence at work. But perhaps more importantly, his relationship with his children blossomed. Freed from the cycle of pain and recovery, he could now be more present and engaged with them, enriching their lives and his own.

This story is a powerful illustration of how changing our approach to health from crisis management to prevention and maintenance can transform lives. It underscores the fact that health is not merely the absence of disease but a state of complete physical, mental, and social well-being. By empowering my clients to take control of their health proactively, I am helping them improve their quality of life and realize their full potential in every aspect of their lives.

A few years back, I experienced something that profoundly shifted my perspective, both personally and professionally. It was just after a tennis game, a routine part of my life, filled with the kind of vigor and competition I thrived on. However, this time, the game left me with a significant shoulder injury, an event that marked the beginning of a challenging journey. The injury was not just a physical setback; it became a barrier to my daily life and work productivity. Simple tasks I had taken for granted, like slipping into a dress shirt or fastening my car seat belt, became sources of intense pain, shooting through my shoulder and arm with the slightest movement.

This ordeal was a humbling experience. It forced me to pause and reflect, providing a stark glimpse into the realities faced by my clients who deal with chronic pain. Before this, I could only empathize with their situations to a certain extent. But living through the constant discomfort and disruption my injury brought to my routine allowed me to understand their struggles on a much deeper level.

Determined to overcome this challenge, I dedicated every spare moment to rehabilitation. I delved into the latest research, seeking innovative biohacks and therapies that promised to expedite the healing process. This period of intense focus was not just about physical recovery but a journey of emotional and mental resilience. I learned to sympathize more deeply with my clients, recognizing how physical pain is often just the tip of the iceberg, with layers of mental and emotional turmoil lying beneath.

This painful lesson was enlightening. It underscored the importance of injury prevention, a principle I had always known but now understood in a new light. The experience taught me that preventing injuries is not merely about avoiding pain; it's about preserving our way of life, our productivity, and our mental well-being. It's about not having to put our lives on hold because of avoidable setbacks.

Since then, I have approached my practice with a renewed focus on prevention, integrating it into my work and advocating for it among my clients. This shift has enhanced my ability to serve them and enriched my personal life, making me more mindful of the need to care for my body and prevent injuries before they occur.

This experience, as challenging as it was, gifted me with valuable insights. It reminded me of the delicate balance between our physical well-being and overall quality of life. It reinforced the importance of prevention, empathy, and the continuous pursuit of knowledge to better serve those in need.

In my journey through the realms of business, I've come to view success not just as a measure of the product, service, or revenue I can generate each month but as a reflection of how well I utilize and invest in my most valuable assets: my physical, emotional, and mental health. This perspective has fundamentally shifted how I approach my work and leadership, emphasizing the importance of a well-rounded investment in oneself to maximize productivity and, ultimately, fulfillment.

I've noticed a trend, particularly among CEOs and leaders, where the emphasis often leans more heavily on IQ—the intellectual prowess one brings to the table—while the significance of EQ, or emotional intelligence, is sometimes undervalued. Yet, in my experience, understanding and nurturing emotional intelligence is crucial. It's about recognizing our emotions and those of others, managing them constructively, and building strong relationships. High EQ is what enables us to lead with empathy, communicate effectively, and navigate the complexities of human dynamics in the business environment.

The corporate world is abundant with material success, a realm where ambition and achievement often take center stage. However, amidst this pursuit, the values of love, appreciation, and compassion can sometimes feel scarce. These are not just soft skills or nice-to-haves; they are the very fabric of a meaningful work environment and the cornerstone of genuine leadership.

I've come to realize that the legacy we leave behind is not measured by the wealth we accumulate or the accolades we receive. Ultimately, we don't take any material possessions with us; the "heart memories" matter most. These are the moments of connection, the acts of kindness, the gestures of appreciation and compassion we share with those around us. In the business context, this means creating a culture that values each individual, fostering an environment where everyone is encouraged to thrive, not just as professionals but as human beings.

Making each moment count is more than a philosophy for life; it's a guiding principle for leadership. It's about being present, engaging fully with the people we work with, and recognizing our impact on their lives and well-being. By prioritizing emotional intelligence and leading with our hearts, we can create a ripple effect of positive change in the corporate world, elevating our businesses and the lives of the people we touch.

In reflecting on my role as a leader, I see it as a privilege and a responsibility to nurture an environment where success is measured not only by what we achieve but also by how we uplift and contribute to the well-being of others. It's a journey of continuous learning and growth, one where investing in ourselves and valuing the power of emotional intelligence can lead us to not just business success but a legacy of love, appreciation, and compassion.

ABOUT THE AUTHOR

Dr. David Yoder is a chiropractic physician specializing in getting to the heart of the matter. He sees the client as a whole person, influenced by epigenetics and lifestyle inputs. You are only a few steps away from achieving your best version of you by identifying main obstacles to health; inflammation, gut microbiome dysbiosis, chronic high cortisol, insomnia, low mitochondrial function and circadian rhythms.

Learn more at davidyoderwellness.com.

Dear Entrepreneur,

Are you looking for a way to take your business to the next level? Writing a co-authored book could be the answer you've been searching for.

As an entrepreneur, you know the importance of building an authoritative presence in your industry. When you co-author a book, it adds instant credibility to your name and opens the door to increased influence and networking opportunities.

That's why SAB Publishing is excited to offer you this unique opportunity. Co-authoring a book with us gives you the chance to become a bestselling author and increase your lead flow. Plus, you'll be able to build your brand and grow your business.

At SAB Publishing, we understand the needs of entrepreneurs like you. That's why we make it easy to write a co-authored book with us. An experienced publisher and editor helps you write a compelling story, as well as professional design and marketing services.

Take the first step to becoming a bestselling author and growing your business.

Contact SAB Publishing today (jetlaunch.link/sp) to learn more about our co-authoring opportunities to grow your business.

Chris O'Byrne
SAB Publishing
books@strategicadvisorboard.com

SAB
PUBLISHING

www.ingramcontent.com/pod-product-compliance
Lightning Source LLC
Chambersburg PA
CBHW060615200326
41521CB00007B/778